OUT TO WIN

THE STORY OF AMERICA IN FRANCE

CONINGSBY DAWSON

1st WORLD
LIBRARY
Literary Society

Out To Win

Coningsby Dawson

© 1st World Library – Literary Society, 2006
PO Box 2211
Fairfield, IA 52556
www.1stworldlibrary.org
First Edition

LCCN: 2006905697

Softcover ISBN: 1-4218-2126-5
Hardcover ISBN: 1-4218-2026-9
eBook ISBN: 1-4218-2226-1

Purchase *"Out To Win"*
as a traditional bound book at:
www.1stWorldLibrary.org/purchase.asp?ISBN=1-4218-2126-5

1st World Library Literary Society is a nonprofit
organization dedicated to promoting literacy by:

- Creating a free internet library accessible from any
computer worldwide.
- Hosting writing competitions and offering book
publishing scholarships.

Out To Win
contributed by Tim, Ed & Rodney
in support of
1st World Library Literary Society

TO

MY AMERICAN FRIENDS AND BROTHERS-
IN-ARMS THIS FRANK APPRECIATION OF
THEIR EFFORT IN FRANCE IS DEDICATED

CONTENTS

A PREFACE FOR FOOLS ONLY

I am not writing this preface for the conscious fool, but for his self-deceived brother who considers himself a very wise person. My hope is that some persons may recognise themselves and be provided with food for thought. They will usually be people who have contributed little to this war, except mean views and endless talk. Had they shared the sacrifice of it, they would have developed within themselves the faculty for a wider generosity. The extraordinary thing about generosity is its eagerness to recognise itself in others.

You find these untravelled critics and mischief-makers on both sides of the Atlantic. In most cases they have no definite desire to work harm, but they have inherited cantankerous prejudices which date back to the American Revolution, and they lack the vision to perceive that this war, despite its horror and tragedy, is the God-given chance of centuries to re-unite the great Anglo-Saxon races of the world in a truer bond of kindness and kinship. If we miss this chance we are flinging in God's face His splendid recompense for our common heroism.

It is an unfortunate fact that the merely foolish person constitutes as grave a danger as the deliberate plotter. His words, if they are acid enough, are quoted and re-quoted. They pass from mouth to mouth, gaining in authority. By the time they reach the friendly country at which they are directed, they have taken on the appearance of an opinion representative of a nation. The Hun is well aware of the value of gossip for the encouraging of divided counsels among his enemies. He invents a slander, pins it to some racial grievance, confides it to the fools among the Allies and leaves them to do the rest. Some of them wander about in a merely private capacity, nagging without knowledge, depositing poison, breeding doubts as to integrity, and all the while pretending to maintain a mildly impartial and judicial mental attitude. Their souls never rise from the ground. Their brains are gangrenous with memories of cancelled malice. They suspect hero-worship; it smacks to them of sentiment. They examine, but never praise. Being incapable of sacrifice, they find something meretriciously melodramatic about men and nations who are capable. Had they lived nineteen hundred years ago, they would have haunted Calvary to discover fraud.

Then, there are others, by far more dangerous. These make their appearance daily in the morning press, thrusting their pessimisms across our breakfast tables, beleaguering our faith with ill-natured judgements and querulous warnings. One of our London Dailies, for instance, specializes in annoying America; it works as effectively to breed distrust as if its policy were dictated from Berlin.

I have just returned from a prolonged tour of America's activities in France. Wherever I went I heard nothing but unstinted appreciation of Great Britain's surpassing gallantry: "We never knew that you Britishers were what you are; you never told us. We had to come over here to find out." When that had been said I always waited, for I guessed the qualifying statement that would follow: "There's only one thing that makes us mad. Why the devil does your censor allow the P - to sneer at us every morning? Your army doesn't feel that way towards us; at least, if it ever did, it doesn't now. Are there really people in England who - ?"

At this point I would cut my questioner short: "There are men so short-sighted in every country that, to warm their hands, they would burn the crown of thorns. You have them in America. Such men are not representative."

The purpose of this book is to tell what America has done, is doing, and, on the strength of her splendid and accomplished facts, to plead for a closer friendship between my two countries. As an Englishman who has lived in the States for ten years and is serving with the Canadian Forces, I feel that I have a sympathetic understanding of the affections and aloofnesses of both nations; as a member of both families I claim the domestic right of indulging in a little plain speaking to each in turn.

In my appeal I leave the fighting men out of the question. Death is a universal teacher of charity. At the end of the war the men who survive will acknowledge no kinship save the kinship of courage. To have answered the call of duty and to have played the man, will make a closer bond than having been born of the same mother. At a New York theatre last October I met some French officers who had fought on the right of the Canadian Corps frontage at the Somme. We got to talking, commenced remembering, missed the entire performance and parted as old friends. In France I stayed with an American-Irish Division. They were for the most part American citizens in the second generation: few of them had been to Ireland. As frequently happens, they were more Irish than the Irish. They had learned from their parents the abuses which had driven them to emigrate, but had no knowledge of the reciprocal provocations which had caused the abuses. Consequently, when they sailed on their troop-ships for France they were anti-British almost to a man - many of them were theoretically Sinn Feiners. They were coming to fight for France and for Lafayette, who had helped to lick Britain - but not for the British. By the time I met them they were marvellously changed. They were going into the line almost any day and - this was what had worked the change - they had been trained for their ordeal by British N.C.O.'s and officers. They had swamped their hatred and inherited bitterness in admiration. Their highest hope was that they might do as well as the British. "They're men if you like," they said. In the imminence of death, their feeling for these old-timers, who had faced death so often, amounted to hero-worship. It was good to hear them deriding the caricature of the typical Briton, which had served in their mental galleries as an exact likeness for so many years. It was proof to me that men who have endured the same hell in a common cause will be nearer in spirit, when the war is ended, than they are to their own civilian populations. For in all belligerent countries there are two armies fighting - the military and the civilian; either can let the other down. If the civilian army loses its *morale*, its vision, its unselfishness, and allows itself to be out-bluffed by the civilian army of Germany, it as surely betrays its soldiers as if it joined forces with the Hun. We execute soldiers for cowardice; it's a pity that the same law does not govern the civilian army. There would be a rapid revision in the tone of more than one English and American newspaper. A soldier is shot for cowardice because his example is contagious. What can be more contagious than a panic statement or a doubt daily reiterated? Already there are many of us who have a kindlier feeling and certainly more respect for a Boche who fights gamely, than for a Britisher or American who bickers and sulks in comfort. Only one doubt as to ultimate victory ever assails the Western Front: that it may be attacked in the rear by the premature peace negotiations of the civil populations it defends. Should that ever happen, the Western Front would cease to be a mixture of French, Americans, Canadians, Australians, British and Belgians; it would become a nation by itself, pledged to fight on till the ideals for which it set out to fight are definitely established.

We get rather tired of reading speeches in which civilians presume that the making of peace is in their hands. The making may be, but the acceptance is in ours. I do not mean that we love war for war's sake. We love it rather less than the civilian does. When an honourable peace has been confirmed, there will be no stauncher pacifist than the soldier; but we reserve our pacifism till the war is won. We shall be the last people in Europe to get war-weary. We started with a vision - the achieving of justice; we shall not grow weary till that vision has become a reality. When one has faced up to an ultimate self-denial, giving becomes a habit. One becomes eager to be allowed to give all - to keep none of life's small change. The fury of an ideal enfevers us. We become fanatical to outdo our own best record in self-surrender. Many of us, if we are alive when peace is declared, will feel an uneasy reproach that perhaps we did not give enough.

This being the spirit of our soldiers, it is easy to understand their contempt for those civilians who go on strike, prate of weariness, scream their terror when a few Hun planes sail over London, devote columns in their papers to pin-prick tragedies of food-shortage, and cloud the growing generosity between England and America by cavilling criticisms and mean reflections. Their contempt is not that of the fighter for the man of peace; but the scorn of the man who is doing his duty for the shirker.

A Tommy is reading a paper in a muddy trench. Suddenly he scowls, laughs rather fiercely and calls to his pal, jerking his head as a sign to him to hurry. "'Ere Bill, listen to wot this 'ere cry-baby says. 'E thinks we're losin' the bloomin' war 'cause 'e didn't get an egg for breakfast. Losin' the war! A lot 'e knows abart it. A blinkin' lot 'e's done either to win or lose it. Yus, I don't think! Thank Gawd, we've none of 'is sort up front."

To men who have gazed for months with the eyes of visionaries on sudden death, it comes as a shock to discover that back there, where life is so sweetly certain, fear still strides unabashed. They had thought that fear was dead - stifled by heroism. They had believed that personal littleness had given way before the magnanimity of martyrdom.

In this plea, then, for a firmer Anglo-American friendship I address the civilian populations of both countries. The fate of such a friendship is in their hands. In the Eden of national destinies God is walking; yet there are those who bray their ancient grievances so loudly that they all but drown the sound of His footsteps.

Being an Englishman it will be more courteous to commence

with the fools of my own flesh and blood. Let me paint a contrast.

Last October I sailed back from New York with a company of American officers; they consisted in the main of trained airmen, Navy experts and engineers. Before my departure the extraordinary sternness of America, her keenness to rival her allies in self-denial, her willing mobilisation of all her resources, had confirmed my optimism gained in the trenches, that the Allies must win; the mere thought of compromise was impossible and blasphemous. This optimism was enhanced on the voyage by the conduct of the officers who were my companions. They carried their spirit of dedication to an excess that was almost irksome. They refused to play cards. They were determined not to relax. Every minute they could snatch was spent in studying text-books. Their country had come into the war so late that they resented any moment lost from making themselves proficient. When expostulated with they explained themselves by saying, "When we've done our bit it will be time to amuse ourselves." They were dull company, but, in a time of war, inspiring. All their talk was of when they reached England. Their enthusiasm for the Britisher was such that they expected to be swept into a rarer atmosphere by the closer contact with heroism.

We had an Englishman with us - obviously a consumptive. He typified for them the doggedness of British pluck. He had been through the entire song and dance of the Mexican Revolution; a dozen times he had been lined up against a wall to be shot. From Mexico he had escaped to New York, hoping to be accepted by the British military authorities. Not unnaturally he had been rejected. The purpose of his voyage to the Old Country was to try his luck with the Navy. He held his certificate as a highly qualified marine engineer. No one could persuade him that he was not wanted. "I could last six months," he said, "it would be something. Heaps of chaps don't last as long."

This man, a crock in every sense, hurrying back to help his

country, symbolised for every American aboard the unconquerable courage of Great Britain. If you hadn't the full measure of years to give, give what was left, even though it were but six months. I may add that in England his services were accepted. His persistence refused to be disregarded. When red-tape stopped his progress, he used back-stairs strategy. No one could bar him from his chance of serving.

In believing that he represented the Empire at its best, my Americans were not mistaken. There are thousands fighting to-day who share his example. One is an ex-champion sculler of Oxford; even in those days he was blind as a bat. His subsequent performance is consistent with his record; we always knew that he had guts. At the start of the war, he tried to enlist and was turned down on the score of eyesight. He tried four times with no better result. The fifth time he presented himself he was fool-proof; he had learnt the eyesight tests by heart. He went out a year ago as a "one pip artist" - a second lieutenant. Within ten months he had become a captain and was acting lieutenant-colonel of his battalion, all the other officers having been killed or wounded. At Cambrai he did such gallant work that he was personally congratulated by the general of his division. These American officers had heard such stories; they regarded England with a kind of worship. As men who hoped to be brave but were untested, they found something mystic and well-nigh incredible in such utter courage. The consumptive racing across the Atlantic that he might do something for England before death took him, made this spirit real to them.

We travelled to London as a party and there for a time we held together. The night before several set out for France, we had a farewell gathering. The consumptive, who had just obtained his commission, was in particularly high feather; he brought with him a friend, a civilian official in the Foreign Office. Please picture the group: all men who had come from distant parts of the world to do one job; men in the army, navy, and flying service; every one in uniform except the stranger.

Talk developed along the line of our absolute certainty as to complete and final victory. The civilian stranger commenced to raise his voice in dissent. We disputed his statements. He then set to work to run through the entire argument of pessimism: America was too far away to be effective; Russia was collapsing; France was exhausted; England had reached the zenith of her endeavour; Italy was not united in purpose. On every front he saw a black cloud rising and took a dyspeptic's delight in describing it as a little blacker than he saw it. There was an apostolic zeal about the man's dreary earnestness. He spoke with that air of authority which is not uncommon with civilian Government officials. The Americans stared rather than listened; this was not the mystic and utter courage which they had expected to find well-nigh incredible. Their own passion far out-topped it.

The argument reached a sudden climax. There were wounded officers present. One of them said, "You wouldn't speak that way if you had the foggiest conception of the kind of chaps we have in the trenches."

"It makes no difference what kind they are," the pessimist replied intolerantly. "I'm asking you to face facts. Because you've succeeded in an attack, you soldiers seem to think that the war is ended. You base your arguments all the time on your little local knowledge of your own particular front."

The discussion ceased abruptly. Every one sprang up. Voices strove together in advising this "facer of facts" to get into khaki and to go to where he could obtain precisely the same kind of little local knowledge - perhaps, a few wounds as well. His presence was dishonourable - contaminating. We filed out and left him sitting humped in a chair, looking puzzled and pathetic, murmuring, "But I thought I was among friends."

My last clear-cut recollection is of a chubby young American Naval Airman standing over him, with clenched fists, passionately instructing him in the spiritual geography of America. That's one type of fool; the type who specialises in catastrophe;

the type who in eternally facing up to facts, takes no account of that magic quality, courage, which can make one man more terrible than an army; the type who is so profoundly well-informed, about externals, that he ignores the mightiness of soul that can remould externals to spiritual purposes. Were I a German, the spectacle of that solitary consumptive leaving the climate which meant life to him and hastening home to give just six months of service to his country, would be more menacing than the loss of an entire corps frontage.

And there's the type who can't forget; he suffers from a fundamental lack of generosity. The Englishman of this type can't refrain from quoting such phrases as, "Too proud to fight," whenever opportunity offers. His American counterpart insists that he is not fighting for Great Britain, but for the French. He makes himself offensive by silly talk about sister republics, implying that all other forms of Government are essentially tyrannic. He never loses an opportunity to mention Lafayette, assuming that one French man is worth ten Britishers. A very gross falsehood is frequently on the lips of this sort of man; he doesn't know where he picked it up and has never troubled to test its accuracy. I can tell him where it originated; at Berlin in the bureau for Hun propaganda. Every time he utters it he is helping the enemy. This falsehood is to the effect that Great Britain has conserved her man-power; that in the early days she let Frenchmen do the fighting and that now she is marking time till Americans are ready to die in her stead. This statement is so stupendously untrue that it goes unheeded by those who know the empty homes of England or have witnessed the gallantry of our piled-up dead.

Then there's the jealous fool - the fool who in England will see no reason why this book should have been published. His line of argument will be, "We've been in this war for more than three years. We've done everything that America is doing; because she's new to the game, we're doing it much better. We don't want any one to appreciate us, so why go praising her?" Precisely. Why be decent? Why seek out affections? Why be polite or kindly? Why not be automatons? I suppose the answer is, "Because we happen to be men, and are privileged temporarily to be playing in the role of heroes. The heroic spirit rather educates one to hold out the hand of friendship to new arrivals of the same sort."

There is one type of fool, exclusively American, whose stupidity arises from love and tenderness. Very often she is a woman. She has been responsible for the arrival in France of a number of narrow-minded and well-intentioned persons; their errand is to investigate vice-conditions in the U.S. Army. This suspicion of the women at home concerning the conduct of their men in the field, is directly traceable to reports of the debasing influences of war set in circulation by the anti-militarists. I want to say emphatically that cleaner, more earnest, better protected troops than those from the United States are not to be found in Europe. Both in Great Britain and on the Continent their puritanism has created a deep impression. By their idealism they have made their power felt; they are men with a vision in their eyes, who have travelled three thousand miles to keep a rendezvous with death. That those for whom they are prepared to die should suspect them is a degrading disloyalty. That trackers should be sent after them from home to pick up clues to their unworthiness is sheerly damnable. To disparage the heroism of other nations is bad enough; to distrust the heroes of your own flesh and blood, attributing to them lower than civilian moral standards, is to be guilty of the meanest treachery and ingratitude.

Here, then, are some of the sample fools to whom this preface is addressed. The list could be indefinitely lengthened. "The fool hath said in his heart, 'There is no God'." He says it in many ways and takes a long while in saying it; but the denying of God is usually the beginning and the end of his conversation. He denies the vision of God in his fellow-men and fellow-nations, even when the spikes of the cross are visibly tearing wounds in their feet and hands.

Life has swung back to a primitive decision since the war commenced. The decision is the same for both men and nations. They can choose the world or achieve their own souls. They can cast mercenary lots for the raiment of a crucified righteousness or take up their martyrdom as disciples. Those men and nations who have been disciples together can scarcely fail to remain friends when the tragedy is ended. What the fool says in his heart at this present is not of any lasting importance. There will always be those who mock, offering vinegar in the hour of agony and taunting, "If thou be what thou sayest...." But in the comradeship of the twilit walk to Emmaus neither the fool nor the mocker are remembered.

I

"WE'VE GOT FOUR YEARS"

The American Troops have set words to one of their bugle calls. These words are indicative of their spirit - of the calculated determination with which they have faced up to their adventure: an adventure unparalleled for magnitude in the history of their nation.

They fall in in two ranks. They tell off from the right in fours. "Move to the right in fours. Quick March," comes the order. The bugles strike up. The men swing into column formation, heads erect and picking up the step. To the song of the bugles they chant words as they march. "We've got four years to do this job. We've got four years to do this job."

That is the spirit of America. Her soldiers give her four years, but to judge from the scale of her preparations she might be planning for thirty.

America is out to win. I write this opening sentence in Paris where I am temporarily absent from my battery, that I may record the story of America's efforts in France. My purpose is to prove with facts that America is in the war to her last dollar, her last man, and for just as long as Germany remains unrepentant. Her strength is unexpended, her spirit is un-war-weary. She has a greater efficient man-power for her population than any nation that has yet entered the arena of hostilities. Her resources are continental rather than national;

Coningsby Dawson

it is as though a new and undivided Europe had sprung to arms in moral horror against Germany. She has this to add fierceness to her soul - the reproach that she came in too late. That reproach is being wiped out rapidly by the scarlet of self-imposed sacrifice. She did come in late - for that very reason she will be the last of Germany's adversaries to withdraw.

She did not want to come in at all. Many of her hundred million population emigrated to her shores out of hatred of militarism and to escape from just such a hell as is now raging in Europe. At first it seemed a far cry from Flanders to San Francisco. Philanthropy could stretch that far, but not the risking of human lives. Moreover, the American nation is not racially a unit; it is bound together by its ideal quest for peaceful and democratic institutions. It was a difficult task for any government to convince so remote a people that their destiny was being made molten in the furnace of the Western Front; when once that truth was fully apprehended the diverse souls of America leapt up as one soul and declared for war. In so doing the people of the United States forewent the freedom from fear that they had gained by their journey across the Atlantic; they turned back in their tracks to smite again with renewed strength and redoubled hate the old brutal Fee-Fo-Fum of despotism, from whose clutches they thought they had escaped.

America's is the case of The Terrible Meek; for two and a half years she lulled Germany and astonished the Allies by her abnormal patience. The most terrifying warriors of history have been peace-loving nations hounded into hostility by outraged ideals. Certainly no nation was ever more peace-loving than the American. To the boy of the Middle West the fury of kings must have read like a fairy-tale. The appeal to armed force was a method of compelling righteousness which his entire training had taught him to view with contempt as obsolete. Yet never has any nation mobilised its resources more efficiently, on so titanic a scale, in so brief a space of time to re-establish justice with armed force. The outraged ideal which achieved this miracle was the denial by the Hun of the right of every man to personal liberty and happiness.

Few people guessed that America would fling her weight so utterly into the winning of the Allied cause. Those who knew her best thought it scarcely possible. Germany, who believed she knew her, thought it least of all. German statesmen argued that America had too much to lose by such a decision - too little to gain; the task of transporting men and materials across three thousand miles of ocean seemed insuperable; the differing traditions of her population would make it impossible for her to concentrate her will in so unusual a direction. Basing their arguments on a knowledge of the deep-seated selfishness of human nature, Hun statesmen were of the fixed opinion that no amount of insult would compel America to take up the sword.

Two and a half years before, those same statesmen made the same mistake with regard to Great Britain and her Dominions. The British were a race of shop-keepers; no matter how chivalrous the call, nothing would persuade them to jeopardise their money-bags. If they did for once leap across their counters to become Sir Galahads, then the Dominions would seize that opportunity to secure their own base safety and to fling the Mother Country out of doors. The British gave these students of selfishness a surprise from which their military machine has never recovered, when the "Old Contemptibles" held up the advance of the Hun legions and won for Europe a breathing-space. The Dominions gave them a second lesson in magnanimity when Canada's lads built a wall with their bodies to block the drive at Ypres. America refuted them for the third time, when she proved her love of world-liberty greater than her affection for the dollar, bugling across the Atlantic her shrill challenge to mailed bestiality. Germany has made the grave mistake of estimating human nature at its lowest worth as she sees it reflected in her own face. In every case, in her judgment of the two great Anglo-Saxon races, she has been at fault through over-emphasising their capacity for baseness and under-estimating their capacity to respond to an ideal. It was an ideal that led the Pilgrim Fathers westward; after more than two hundred years it is an ideal which pilots their sons home again, racing through danger zones in their steel-built greyhounds that they may lay down their lives in France.

In view of the monumental stupidity of her diplomacy Germany has found it necessary to invent explanations. The form these have taken as regards America has been the attributing of fresh low motives. Her object at first was to prove to the world at large how very little difference America's participation in hostilities would make. When America tacitly negatived this theory by the energy with which she raised billions and mobilised her industries, Hun propagandists, by an ingenious casuistry, spread abroad the opinion that these mighty preparations were a colossal bluff which would redound to Germany's advantage. They said that President Wilson had bided his time so that his country might strut as a belligerent for only the last six months, and so obtain a voice in the peace negotiations. He did not intend that America should fight, and was only getting his armies ready that they might enforce peace when the Allies were exhausted and already counting on Americans manning their trenches. Inasmuch as his country would neither have sacrificed nor died, he would be willing to give Germany better terms; therefore America's apparent joining of the Allies was a camouflage which would turn out an advantage to Germany. This lie, with variations, has spread beyond the Rhine and gained currency in certain of the neutral nations.

Four days after President Wilson's declaration of war the Canadians captured Vimy Ridge. As the Hun prisoners came running like scared rabbits through the shell-fire, we used to question them as to conditions on their side of the line. Almost the first question that was asked was, "What do you think about the United States?" By far the most frequent reply was, "We have submarines; the United States will make no difference." The answer was so often in the same formula that it was evident the men had been schooled in the opinion. It was only the rare man of education who said, "It is bad - very bad; the worst mistake we have made."

We, in the front-line, were very far from appreciating America's decision at its full value. For a year we had had the upper-hand of the Hun. To use the language of the trenches, we knew that we could go across No Man's Land and "beat him up" any time we liked. To tell the truth, many of us felt a little jealous that when, after two years of punishment, we had at last become top-dog, we should be called upon to share the glory of victory with soldiers of the eleventh hour. We believed that we were entirely capable of finishing the job without further aid. My own feeling, as an Englishman living in New York, was merely one of relief - that now, when war was ended, I should be able to return to friends of whom I need not be ashamed. To what extent America's earnestness has changed that sentiment is shown by the expressed desire of every Canadian, that if Americans are anywhere on the Western Front, they ought to be next to us in the line. "They are of our blood," we say; "they will carry on our record." Only those who have had the honour to serve with the Canadian Corps and know its dogged adhesion to heroic traditions, can estimate the value of this compliment.

I should say that in the eyes of the combatant, after President Wilson, Mr. Ford has done more than any other one man to interpret the spirit of his nation; our altered attitude towards him typifies our altered attitude towards America. Mr. Ford, the impassioned pacifist, sailing to Europe in his ark of peace, staggered our amazement. Mr. Ford, still the impassioned pacifist, whose aeroplane engines will help to bomb the Hun's conscience into wakefulness, staggers our amazement but commands our admiration. We do not attempt to understand or reconcile his two extremes of conduct, but as fighters we appreciate the courage of soul that made him "about turn" to search for his ideal in a painful direction when the old friendly direction had failed. Here again it is significant that both with regard to individuals and nations, Germany's sternest foes are war-haters - war-haters to such an extent that their principles at times have almost shipwrecked their careers. In England our example is Lloyd George. Throughout the Anglo-Saxon world the slumbering spirit of Cromwell's Ironsides has sprung to life, reminding the British Empire and the United States of their common ancestry. After a hundred and forty years of drifting apart, we stand side by side like our forefathers, the fighting pacifists at Naseby; like them, having failed to make men good with words, we will hew them into virtue with the sword.

At the end of June I went back to Blighty wounded. One of my most vivid recollections of the time that followed is an early morning in July; it must have been among the first of the days that I was allowed out of hospital. London was green and leafy. The tracks of the tramways shone like silver in the sunlight. There was a spirit of release and immense good humour abroad. My course followed the river on the south side, all a-dance with wind and little waves. As I crossed the bridge at Westminster I became aware of an atmosphere of expectation. Subconsciously I must have been noticing it for some time. Along Whitehall the pavements were lined with people, craning their necks, joking and jostling, each trying to better his place. Trafalgar Square was jammed with a dense mass of humanity, through which mounted police pushed their way solemnly, like beadles in a vast unroofed cathedral. Then for the first time I noticed what I ought to have noticed long before, that the Stars and Stripes were exceptionally prevalent. Upon inquiry I was informed that this was the day on which the first of the American troops were to march. I picked up with a young officer or the Dublin Fusiliers and together we forced our way down Pall Mall to the office of The Cecil Rhodes Oxford Scholars' Foundation. From here we could watch the line of march from Trafalgar Square to Marlborough House. While we waited, I scanned the group-photographs on the walls, some of which contained portraits of German Rhodes Scholars with whom I had been acquainted. I remembered how they had always spent their vacations in England, assiduously bicycling to the most unexpected places. In the light of later developments I thought I knew the reason.

Suddenly, far away bands struck up. We thronged the windows, leaning out that we might miss nothing. Through the half mile of people that stretched between us and the music a shudder of excitement was running. Then came cheers - the deep-throated babel of men's voices and the shrill staccato of women's. "They're coming," some one cried; then I saw them.

I forget which regiment lead. The Coldstreams were there, the Scotch and Welsh Guards, the Irish Guards with their saffron kilts and green ribbons floating from their bag-pipes. A British regimental band marched ahead of each American regiment to do it honour. Down the sunlit canyon of Pall Mall they swung to the tremendous cheering of the crowd. Quite respectable citizens had climbed lamp-posts and railings, and were waving their hats. I caught the words that were being shouted, "Are we downhearted?" Then, in a fierce roar of denial, "No!" It was a wonderful ovation - far more wonderful than might have been expected from a people who had grown accustomed to the sight of troops during the last three years. The genuineness of the welcome was patent; it was the voice of England that was thundering along the pavements.

I was anxious to see the quality of the men which America had sent. They drew near; then I saw them plainly. They were fine strapping chaps, broad of shoulder and proudly independent. They were not soldiers yet; they were civilians who had been rushed into khaki. Their equipment was of every kind and sort and spoke eloquently of the hurry in which they had been brought together. That meant much to us in London-much more than if they had paraded with all the "spit and polish" of the crack troops who led them. It meant to us that America was doing her bit at the earliest date possible.

The other day, here in France, I met an officer of one of those battalions; he told me the Americans' side of the story. They were expert railroad troops, picked out of civilian life and packed off to England without any pretence at military training. When they were informed that they were to be the leading feature in a London procession, many of them even lacked uniforms. With true American democracy of spirit, the officers stripped their rank-badges from their spare tunics and lent them to the privates, who otherwise could not have marched.

"I'm satisfied," my friend said, "that there were Londoners so doggone hoarse that night that they couldn't so much as whisper."

What impressed the men most of all was the King's friendly greeting of them at Buckingham Palace. There were few of them who had ever seen a king before. "Friendly - that's the word! From the King downwards they were all so friendly. It was more like a family party than a procession; and on the return journey, when we marched at ease, old ladies broke up our formations to kiss us. Nice and grandmotherly of them we thought."

This, as I say, I learnt later in France; at the time I only knew that the advance-guard of millions was marching. As I watched them my eyes grew misty. Troops who have already fought no longer stir me; they have exchanged their dreams of glory for the reality of sacrifice - they know to what they may look forward. But untried troops have yet to be disillusioned; dreams of the pomp of war are still in their eyes. They have not yet owned that they are merely going out to die obscurely.

That day made history. It was then that England first vividly realised that America was actually standing shoulder to shoulder at her side. In making history it obliterated almost a century and a half of misunderstanding. I believe I am correct in saying that the last foreign troops to march through London were the Hessians, who fought against America in the Revolution, and that never before had foreign volunteers marched through England save as conquerors.

On my recovery I was sent home on sick leave and spent a month in New York. No one who has not been there since America joined the Allies can at all realise the change that has taken place. It is a change of soul, which no statistics of armaments can photograph. America has come into the war not only with her factories, her billions and her man-power, but with her heart shining in her eyes. All her spread-eagleism is gone. All her aggressive industrial ruthlessness has vanished. With these has been lost her youthful contempt for older civilisations, whom she was apt to regard as decaying because they sent her emigrants. She has exchanged her prejudices for admiration and her grievances for kindness. Her "Hats off" attitude to France, England, Belgium and to every nation that has shed blood for the cause which now is hers, was a thing which I had scarcely expected; it was amazing. As an example of how this attitude is being interpreted into action, school-histories throughout the United States are being re-written, so that American children of the future may be trained in friendship for Great Britain, whereas formerly stress was laid on the hostilities of the eighteenth century which produced the separation. As a further example, many American boys, who for various reasons were not accepted by the military authorities in their own country, have gone up to Canada to join.

One such case is typical. Directly it became evident that America was going into the war, one boy, with whom I am acquainted, made up his mind to be prepared to join. He persuaded his father to allow him to go to a Flying School to train as a pilot. Having obtained his certificate, he presented himself for enlistment and was turned down on the ground that he was lacking in a sense of equipoise. Being too young for any other branch of the service, he persuaded his family to allow him to try his luck in Canada. Somehow, by hook or by crook, he had to get into the war. The Royal Flying Corps accepted him with the proviso that he must take out his British naturalisation papers. This changing of nationality was a most bitter pill for his family to swallow. The boy had done his best to be a soldier; he was the eldest son, and there they would willingly have had the matter rest. Moreover they could compel the matter to rest there, for, being under age, he could not change his nationality without his father's consent. It was his last desperate argument that turned the decision in his favour, "If it's a choice between my honour and my country, I choose my honour every time." So now he's a Britisher, learning "spit and polish" and expecting to bring down a Hun almost any day.

One noticed in almost the smallest details how deeply America had committed her conscience to her new undertaking. While in England we grumble about a food-control which is absolutely necessary to our preservation, America is voluntarily restricting herself not for her own sake, but for the sake of the Allies. They say that they are being "Hooverized," thus coining a new word out of Mr. Hoover's name. Sometimes these Hooverish practices produce contrasts which are rather quaint. I went to stay with a friend who had just completed as his home an exact reproduction of a palace in Florence. Whoever went short, there was little that he could not afford. At our meals I noticed that I was the only person who was served with butter and sugar, and enquired why. "It's all right for you," I was told; "you're a soldier; but if we eat butter and sugar, some of the Allies who really need them will have to go short." A small illustration, but one that is typical of a national, sacrificial, underlying thought.

Later I met with many instances of the various forms in which this thought is taking shape. I was in America when the Liberty War Loan was so amazingly over-subscribed. I saw buses, their roofs crowded with bands and orators, doing the tour of street-corners. Every store of any size, every railroad, every bank and financial corporation had set for its employes and customers the ideal sum which it considered that they personally ought to subscribe. This ideal sum was recorded on the face of a clock, hung outside the building. As the gross amount actually collected increased, the hands were seen to revolve. Everything that eloquence and ingenuity could devise was done to gather funds for the war. Big advertisers made a gift of their newspaper space to the nation. There were certain public-spirited men who took up blocks of war-bonds, making the request that no interest should be paid. You went to a theatre; during the interval actors and actresses sold war-certificates, harangued the audience and set the example by their own purchases.

When the Liberty War Loan had been raised, the Red Cross started its great national drive, apportioning the necessary grand total among all the cities from sea-board to sea-board, according to their wealth and population.

One heard endless stories of the variety of efforts being made. America had committed her heart to the Allies with an abandon which it is difficult to describe. Young society girls, who had been brought up in luxury and protected from ugliness all their lives, were banding themselves into units, supplying the money, hiring the experts, and coming over themselves to France to look after refugees' babies. Others were planning to do reconstruction work in the devastated districts immediately behind the battle-line. I met a number of these enthusiasts before they sailed; I have since seen them at work in France. What struck me at the time was their rose-leaf frailness and utter unsuitability for the task. I could guess the romantic visions which tinted their souls to the colour of sacrifice; I also knew what refugees and devastated districts look like. I feared that the discrepancy between the dream and the reality would doom them to disillusion.

During the month that I was in America I visited several of the camps. The first draft army had been called. The first call gave the country seven million men from which to select. I was surprised to find that in many camps, before military training could commence, schools in English had to be started to ensure the men's proper understanding of commands. This threw a new light on the difficulties Mr. Wilson had had to face in coming into the war.

The men of the draft army represent as many nationalities, dialects and race-prejudices as there are in Europe. They are a Europe expatriated. During their residence in America a great many of them have lived in communities where their own language is spoken, and their own customs are maintained. Frequently they have their own newspapers, which foster their national exclusiveness, and reflect the hatreds and affections of the country from which they emigrated. These conditions set up a barrier between them and current American opinion which it was difficult for the authorities at Washington to cross. The people who represented neutral European nations naturally were anxious for the neutrality of America. The people who represented the Central Powers naturally were against America siding with the Allies. The only way of re-directing their sympathies was by means of education and propaganda; this took time, especially when they were separated from the truth by the stumbling block of language. For three years they had to be persuaded that they were no longer Poles, Swedes, Germans, Finns, Norwegians, but first and last Americans. I mention this here, in connection with the teaching of the draft army English, because it affords one of the most vivid and comprehensible reasons for America's long delay.

What brought America into the war? I have often been asked the question; in answering it I always feel that I am giving only a partial answer. On the one hand there is the record of her two and a half years of procrastination, on the other the titanic upspringing of her warrior-spirit, which happened almost in a day. How can one reconcile the multitudinous pacific notes which issued from Washington with the bugle-song to which the American boys march: "We've got four years to do this job." The cleavage between the two attitudes is too sharp for the comprehension of other nations.

The first answer which I shall give is entirely sane and will be accepted by the rankest cynic. America came into the war at the moment she realised that her own national life was endangered. Her leaders realised this months before her masses could be persuaded. The political machinery of the United States is such that no Government would dare to commence hostilities unless it was assured that its decision was the decision of the entire nation. That the Government might have this assurance, Mr. Wilson had to maintain peace long after the intellect of America had declared for war, while he educated the cosmopolitan citizenship of his country into a knowledge of Hun designs. The result was that he created the appearance of having been pushed into hostilities by the weight of public opinion.

For many months the Secret Service agents of the States, aided by the agents of other nations, were unravelling German plots and collecting data of treachery so irrefutable that it had to be accepted. When all was ready the first chapters of the story were divulged. They were divulged almost in the form of a serial novel, so that the man who read his paper to-day and said, "No doubt that isolated item is true, but it doesn't incriminate the entire German nation," next day on opening his paper, found further proof and was forced to retreat to more ingenious excuses. One day he was informed of Germany's abuse of neutral embassies and mail-bags; the next of the submarine bases in Mexico, prepared as a threat against American shipping; the day after that the whole infamous story of how Berlin had financed the Mexican Revolution. Germany's efforts to provoke an American-Japanese war leaked out, her attempts to spread disloyalty among German-Americans, her conspiracies for setting fire to factories and powder-plants, including the blowing up of bridges and the Welland Canal. Quietly, circumstantially, without rancour, the details were published of the criminal spider-web woven by the Dernburgs, Bernstorffs and Von Papens, accredited creatures of the Kaiser, who with Machiavellian smiles had professed friendship for those whom their hands itched to slay and strangle. Gradually the camouflage of bovine geniality was lifted from the face of Germany and the dripping fangs of the Blonde Beast were displayed - the Minotaur countenance of one glutted with human flesh, weary with rape and rapine, but still tragically insatiable and lusting for the new sensation of hounding America to destruction.

I have not placed these revelations in their proper sequence; some were made after war had been declared. They had the effect of changing every decent American into a self-appointed detective. The weight of evidence put Germany's perfidy beyond dispute; clues to new and endless chains of machinations were discovered daily. The Hun had come as a guest into America's house with only one intent - to do murder as soon as the lights were out.

The anger which these disclosures produced knew no bounds. Hun apologists - the type of men who invariably believe that there is a good deal to be said on both sides - quickly faded into patriots. There had been those who had cried out for America's intervention from the first day that Belgium's neutrality had been violated. Many of these, losing patience, had either enlisted in Canada or were already in France on some errand of mercy. Their cry had reached Washington at first only as a whisper, very faint and distant. Little by little that cry had swelled, till it became the nation's voice, angry, insistent, not to be disregarded. The most convinced humanitarian, together with the sincerest admirer of the old-fashioned kindly Hans, had to join in that cry or brand himself a traitor by his silence.

America came into the war, as every country came, because her life was threatened. She is not fighting for France, Great Britain, Belgium, Serbia; she is fighting to save herself. I am glad to make this point because I have heard camouflaged Pro-Germans and thoughtless mischief-makers discriminating between the Allies. "We are not fighting for Great Britain," they say, "but for plucky France." When I was in New York last October a firm stand was being made against these discriminators; some of them even found themselves in the hands of the Secret Service men. The feeling was growing that not to be Pro-British was not to be Pro-Ally, and that not to be Pro-Ally was to be anti-American. This talk of fighting for somebody else is all lofty twaddle. America is fighting for America. While the statement is perfectly true, Americans have a right to resent it.

In September, 1914, I crossed to Holland and was immensely disgusted at the interpretation of Great Britain's action which I found current there. I had supposed that Holland would be full of admiration; I found that she was nothing of the sort. We Britishers, in those early days, believed that we were magnanimous big brothers who could have kept out of the bloodshed, but preferred to die rather than see the smaller nations bullied. Men certainly did not join Kitchener's mob because they believed that England's life was threatened. I don't believe that any strong emotion of patriotism animated Canada in her early efforts. The individual Briton donned the khaki because he was determined to see fair play, and was damned if he would stand by a spectator while women and children were being butchered in Belgium. He felt that he had to do something to stop it. If he didn't, the same thing would happen in Holland, then in Denmark, then in Norway. There was no end to it. When a mad dog starts running the best thing to do is to shoot it.

But the Hollanders didn't agree with me at all. "You're fighting for yourselves," they said. "You're not fighting to save us from being invaded; you're not fighting to prevent the Hun from conquering France; you're not fighting to liberate Belgium. You're fighting because you know that if you let France be crushed, it will be your turn next."

Quite true - and absolutely unjust. The Hollander, whose households we were guarding, chose to interpret our motive at its most ignoble worth. Our men were receiving in their bodies the wounds which would have been inflicted on Holland, had we elected to stand out. In the light of subsequent events, all the world acknowledges that we were and are fighting for our own households; but it is a glorious certainty that scarcely a Britisher who died in those early days had the least realisation of the fact. It was the chivalrous vision of a generous Crusade that led our chaps from their firesides to the trampled horror that is Flanders. They said farewell to their habitual affections, and went out singing to their marriage with death.

I suppose there has been no war that could not be interpreted ultimately as a war of self-interest. The statesmen who make wars always carefully reckon the probabilities of loss or gain;

but the lads who kiss their sweethearts good-bye require reasons more vital than those of pounds, shillings and pence. Few men lay down their lives from self-interested motives. Courage is a spiritual quality which requires a spiritual inducement. Men do not set a price on their chance of being blown to bits by shells. Even patriotism is too vague to be a sufficient incentive. The justice of the cause to be fought for helps; it must be proportionate to the magnitude of the sacrifice demanded. But always an ideal is necessary - an ideal of liberty, indignation and mercy. If this is true of the men who go out to die, it is even more true of the women who send them,

"Where there're no children left to pull
The few scared, ragged flowers -
All that was ours, and, God, how beautiful!
All, all that was once ours,
Lies faceless, mouthless, mire to mire,
So lost to all sweet semblance of desire
That we, in those fields seeking desperately
One face long-lost to love, one face that lies
Only upon the breast of Memory,
Would never find it - even the very blood
Is stamped into the horror of the mud -
Something that mad men trample under-foot
In the narrow trench - for these things are not men -
Things shapeless, sodden, mute
Beneath the monstrous limber of the guns;
Those things that loved us once...
Those that were ours, but never ours again."

For two and a half years the American press specialized on the terror aspect of the European hell. Every sensational, exceptional fact was not only chronicled, but widely circulated. The bodily and mental havoc that can be wrought by shell fire was exaggerated out of all proportion to reality. Photographs, almost criminal in type, were published to illustrate the brutal expression of men who had taken part in bayonet charges. Lies were spread broadcast by supposedly reputable persons, stating how soldiers had to be maddened with drugs or alcohol before they would go over the top. Much of what was recorded was calculated to stagger the imagination and intimidate the heart. The reason for this was that the supposed eye-witnesses rarely saw what they recorded. They had usually never been within ten miles of the front, for only combatants are allowed in the line. They brought civilian minds, undisciplined to the conquest of fear, to their task; they never for one instant guessed the truly spiritual exaltation which gives wings to the soul of the man who fights in a just cause. Squalor, depravity, brutalisation, death - moral, mental and physical deformity were the rewards which the American public learned the fighting man gained in the trenches. They heard very little of the capacity for heroism, the eagerness for sacrifice, the gallant self-effacement which having honor for a companion taught. And yet, despite this frantic portrayal of terror, America decided for war. Her National Guard and Volunteers rolled up in millions, clamouring to cross the three thousand miles of water that they might place their lives in jeopardy. They were no more urged by motives of self-interest than were the men who enlisted in Kitchener's mob. It wasn't the threat to their national security that brought them; it was the lure of an ideal - the fine white knightliness of men whose compassion had been tormented and whose manhood had been challenged. When one says that America came into the war to save herself it is only true of her statesmen; it is no more true of her masses than it was true of the masses of Great Britain.

So far, in my explanation as to why America came into the war, I have been scarcely more generous in the attributing of magnanimous motives than my Hollander. To all intents and purposes I have said, "America is fighting because she knows that if the Allies are over-weakened or crushed, it will be her turn next." In discussing the matter with me, one of our Generals said, "I really don't see that it matters a tuppenny cuss why she's fighting, so long as she helps us to lick the Hun and does it quickly." But it does matter. The reasons for her having taken up arms make all the difference to our respect for her. Here, then, are the reasons which I attribute: enthusiasm

Coningsby Dawson

for the ideals of the Allies; admiration for the persistency of their heroism; compassionate determination to borrow some of the wounds which otherwise would be inflicted upon nations which have already suffered. A small band of pioneers in mercy are directly responsible for this change of attitude in two and a half years from opportunistic neutrality to a reckless welcoming of martyrdom.

At the opening of hostilities in 1914, America divided herself into two camps - the Pro-Allies and the others. "The others" consisted of people of all shades of opinion and conviction: the anti-British, anti-French, the pro-German, the anti-war and the merely neutral, some of whom set feverishly to work to make a tradesman's advantage out of Europe's misfortune. A great traffic sprang up in the manufacture of war materials. Almost all of these went to the Allies, owing to the fact that Britain controlled the seas. Whether they would not have been sold just as readily to Germany, had that been possible, is a matter open to question. In any case, the camp of "The Others" was overwhelmingly in the majority.

One by one, and in little protesting bands, the friends of the Allies slipped overseas bound on self-imposed, sacrificial quests. They went like knight-errants to the rescue; while others suffered, their own ease was intolerable. The women, whom they left, formed themselves into groups for the manufacture of the munitions of mercy. There were men like Alan Seeger, who chanced to be in Europe when war broke out; many of these joined up with the nearest fighting units. "I have a rendezvous with death," were Alan Seeger's last words as he fell mortally wounded between the French and German trenches. His voice was the voice of thousands who had pledged themselves to keep that rendezvous in the company of Britishers, Belgians and Frenchmen, long before their country had dreamt of committing herself. Some of these friends of the Allies chose the Ford Ambulance, others positions in the Commission for the Relief of Belgium, and yet others the more forceful sympathy of the bayonet as a means of expressing their wrath. Soon, through the heart of France, with the tricolor and the Stars and Stripes flying at either end, "le train Americaine" was seen hurrying, carrying its scarlet burden. This sight could hardly be called neutral unless a similar sight could be seen in Germany. It could not. The Commission for the Relief of Belgium was actually anything but neutral; to minister to the results of brutality is tacitly to condemn.

At Neuilly-sur-Seine the American Ambulance Hospital sprang up. It undertook the most grievous cases, making a specialty of facial mutilations. American girls performed the nursing of these pitiful human wrecks. Increasingly the crusader spirit was finding a gallant response in the hearts of America's girlhood. By the time that President Wilson flung his challenge, eighty-six war relief organizations were operating in France. In very many cases these organizations only represented a hundredth part of the actual personnel working; the other ninety-nine hundredths were in the States, rolling bandages, shredding oakum, slitting linen, making dressings. Long before April, 1917, American college boys had won a name by their devotion in forcing their ambulances over shell torn roads on every part of the French Front, but, perhaps, with peculiar heroism at Verdun. Already the American Flying Squadron has earned a veteran's reputation for its daring. The report of the sacrificial courage of these pioneers had travelled to every State in the Union; their example had stirred, shamed and educated the nation. It is to these knight-errants - very many of them boys and girls in years - to the Mrs. Whartons, the Alan Seegers, the Hoovers and the Thaws that I attribute America's eager acceptance of Calvary, when at last it was offered to her by her Statesmen. From an anguished horror to be repelled, war had become a spiritual Eldorado in whose heart lay hidden the treasure-trove of national honor.

The individual American soldier is inspired by just as altruistic motives as his brother-Britisher. Compassion, indignation, love of justice, the determination to see right conquer are his incentives. You can make a man a conscript, drill him, dress him in uniform, but you cannot force him to face up to four years to do his job unless the ideals were there beforehand. I have seen American troop-ships come into the dock with ten thousand men singing,

"Good-bye, Liza,
I'm going to smash the Kaiser."

I have been present when packed audiences have gone mad in reiterating the American equivalent for *Tipperary*, with its brave promise,

"We'll be over,
We're coming over,
And we won't be back till it's over, over there."

But nothing I have heard so well expresses the cold anger of the American fighting-man as these words which they chant to their bugle-march, "We've got four years to do this job."

II

WAR AS A JOB

I have been so fortunate as to be able to watch three separate nations facing up to the splendour of Armageddon - England, France, America. The spirit of each was different. I arrived in England from abroad the week after war had been declared. There was a new vitality in the air, a suppressed excitement, a spirit of youth and - it sounds ridiculous - of opportunity. The England I had left had been wont to go about with a puckered forehead; she was a victim of self-disparagement. She was like a mother who had borne too many children and was at her wits' end to know how to feed or manage them. They were getting beyond her control. Since the Boer War there had been a growing tendency in the Press to under-rate all English effort and to over-praise to England's discredit the superior pushfulness of other nations. This melancholy nagging which had for its constant text, "Wake up, John Bull," had produced the hallucination that there was something vitally the matter with the Mother Country. No one seemed to have diagnosed her complaint, but those of us who grew weary of being told that we were behind the times, took prolonged trips to more cheery quarters of the globe. It is the Englishman's privilege to run himself down; he usually does it with his tongue in his cheek. But for the ten years preceding the outbreak of hostilities, the prophets of Fleet Street certainly carried their privilege beyond a joke. Pessimism was no longer an amusing pose; it was becoming a habit.

One week of the iron tonic of war had changed all that. The atmosphere was as different as the lowlands from the Alps; it was an atmosphere of devil-may-care assurance and adventurous manhood. Every one had the summer look of a boat-race crowd when the Leander is to be pulled off at Henley. In comparing the new England with the old, I should have said that every one now had the comfortable certainty that he was wanted - that he had a future and something to live for. But it wasn't the something to live for that accounted for this gay alertness; it was the sure foreknowledge of each least important man that he had something worth dying for at last.

A strange and magnificent way of answering misfortune's challenge - an Elizabethan way, the knack of which we believed we had lost! "Business as usual" was written across our doorways. It sounded callous and unheeding, but at night the lads who had written it there, tiptoed out and stole across the Channel, scarcely whispering for fear they should break our hearts by their going.

Death may be regarded as a funeral or as a Columbus expedition to worlds unknown - it may be seized upon as an opportunity for weeping or for a display of courage. From the first day in her choice England never hesitated; like a boy set free from school, she dashed out to meet her danger with laughter. Her high spirits have never failed her. Her cavalry charge with hunting-calls upon their lips. Her Tommies go over the top humming music-hall ditties. The Hun is still "jolly old Fritz." The slaughter is still "a nice little war." Death is still "the early door." The mud-soaked "old Bills" of the trenches, cheerfully ignoring vermin, rain and shell fire, continue to wind up their epistles with, "Hoping this finds you in the pink, as it leaves me at present." They are always in the pink for epistolary purposes, whatever the strafing or the weather. That's England; at all costs, she has to be a sportsman. I wonder she doesn't write on the crosses above her dead, "*Yours in the pink: a British soldier, killed in action.*" England is in the pink for the duration of the war.

The Frenchman cannot understand us, and I don't blame him. Our high spirits impress him as untimely and indecent. War for him is not a sport. How could it be, with his homesteads ravaged, his cities flattened, his women violated, his populations prisoners in occupied territories? For him war is a martyrdom which he embraces with a fierce gladness. His spirit is well illustrated by an incident that happened the other day in Paris. A descendant of Racine, a well-known figure at the opera, was travelling in the Metro when he spotted a poilu with a string of ten medals on his breast. The old aristocrat went over to the soldier and apologised for speaking to him. "But," he said, "I have never seen any poilu with so many decorations. You must be of the very bravest."

"That is nothing," the man replied sombrely; "before they kill me I shall have won many more. This I earned in revenge for my wife, who was brutally murdered. And this and this and this for my daughters who were ravished. And these others - they are for my sons who are now no more."

"My friend, if you will let me, I should like to embrace you." And there, in the sight of all the passengers, the old habitue of the opera and the common soldier kissed each other. The one satisfaction that the French blind have is in counting the number of Boche they have slaughtered. "In that raid ten of us killed fifty," one will say; "the memory makes me very happy."

Curiously enough the outrage that makes the Frenchman most revengeful is not the murder of his family or the defilement of his women, but the wilful killing of his land and orchards. The land gave birth to all his flesh and blood; when his farm is laid waste wilfully, it is as though the mother of all his generations was violated. This accounts for the indomitable way in which the peasants insist on staying on in their houses under shell-fire, refusing to depart till they are forcibly turned out.

We in England, still less in America, have never approached the loathing which is felt for the Boche in France. Men spit as they utter his name, as though the very word was foul in the mouth.

In the face of all that they have suffered, I do not wonder that the French misunderstand the easy good-humour with which we English go out to die. In their eyes and with the continual throbbing of their wounds, this war is an occasion for neither good-humour nor sportsmanship, but for the wrath of a Hebrew Jehovah, which only blows can appease or make articulate. If every weapon were taken from their hands and all their young men were dead, with naked fists those who were left would smite - smite and smite. It is fitting that they should feel this way, seeing themselves as they do perpetually frescoed against the sky-line of sacrifice; but I am glad that our English boys can laugh while they die.

In trying to explain the change I found in England after war had commenced, I mentioned Henley and the boat-race crowds. I don't think it was a change; it was only a bringing to the surface of something that had been there always. Some years ago I was at Henley when the Belgians carried off the Leander Cup from the most crack crew that England could bring together. Evening after evening through the Regatta week the fear had been growing that we should lose, yet none of that fear was reflected in our attitude towards our Belgian guests. Each evening as they came up the last stretch of river, leading by lengths and knocking another contestant out, the spectators cheered them madly. Their method of rowing smashed all our traditions; it wasn't correct form; it wasn't anything. It ought to have made one angry. But these chaps were game; they were winning. "Let's play fair," said the river; so they cheered them. On the last night when they beat Leander, looking fresh as paint, leading by a length and taking the championship out of England, you would never have guessed by the flicker of an eyelash that it wasn't the most happy conclusion of a good week's sport for every oarsman present.

It's the same spirit essentially that England is showing to-day. She cheers the winner. She trusts in her strength for another day. She insists on playing fair. She considers it bad manners to lose one's temper. She despises to hate back. She has carried this spirit so far that if you enter the college chapels of Oxford to-day, you will find inscribed on memorial tablets to the fallen not only the names of Britishers, but also the names of German Rhodes Scholars, who died fighting for their country against the men who were once their friends. Generosity, justice, disdain of animosity-these virtues were learnt on the playing-fields and race-courses. England knows their value; she treats war as a sport because so she will fight better. For her that approach to adversity is normal.

With us war is a sport. With the French it is a martyrdom. But with the Americans it is a job. "We've got four years to do this job. We've got four years to do this job," as the American soldiers chant. I think in these three attitudes towards war as a martyrdom, as sport and as a job, you get reflected the three gradations of distance by which each nation is divided from the trenches. France had her tribulation thrust upon her. She was attacked; she had no option. England, separated by the Channel, could have restrained the weight of her strength, biding her time. She had her moment of choice, but rushed to the rescue the moment the first Hun bayonet gleamed across the Belgian threshold. America, fortified by the Atlantic, could not believe that her peace was in any way assailed. The idea seemed too madly far-fetched. At first she refused to realise that this apportioning of a continent three thousand miles distant from Germany was anything but a pipe-dream of diplomats in their dotage. It was inconceivable that it could be the practical and achievable cunning of military bullies and strategists. The truth dawned too slowly for her to display any vivid burst of anger. "It isn't true," she said. And then, "It seems incredible." And lastly, "What infernal impertinence!"

It was the infernal impertinence of Germany's schemes for transatlantic plunder that roused the average American. It awoke in him a terrible, calm anger - a feeling that some one must be punished. It was as though he broke off suddenly in what he was doing and commenced rolling up his shirt-sleeves.

There was a grim, surprised determination about his quietness, which had not been seen in any other belligerent nation. France became consciously and tragically heroic when war commenced. England became unwontedly cheerful because life was moving on grander levels. In America there was no outward change. The old habit of feverish industry still persisted, but was intensified and applied in unselfish directions.

What has impressed me most in my tour of the American activities in France is the businesslike relentlessness of the preparations. Everything is being done on a titanic scale and everything is being done to last. The ports, the railroads, the plants that are being constructed will still be standing a hundred years from now. There's no "Home for Christmas" optimism about America's method of making war. One would think she was expecting to be still fighting when all the present generation is dead. She is investing billions of dollars in what can only be regarded as permanent improvements. The handsomeness of her spirit is illustrated by the fact that she has no understanding with the French for reimbursement.

In sharp contrast with this handsomeness of spirit is the iciness of her purpose as regards the Boche. I heard no hatred of the individual German - only the deep conviction that Prussianism must be crushed at all costs. The American does not speak of "Poor old Fritz" as we do on our British Front. He's too logical to be sorry for his enemy. His attitude is too sternly impersonal for him to be moved by any emotions, whether of detestation or charity, as regards the Hun. All he knows is that a Frankenstein machinery has been set in motion for the destruction of the world; to counteract it he is creating another piece of machinery. He has set about his job in just the same spirit that he set about overcoming the difficulties of the Panama Canal. He has been used to overcoming the obstinacies of Nature; the human obstinacies of his new task intrigue him. I believe that, just as in peace times big business was his romance and the wealth which he gained from it was often incidental, so in France the job as a job impels him, quite apart from its heroic object. After all, smashing the Pan-Germanic Combine is only another form of trust-busting - trust-busting with aeroplanes and guns instead of with law and ledgers.

There is something almost terrifying to me about this quiet collectedness - this Pierpont Morgan touch of sphinxlike aloofness from either malice or mercy. Just as America once said, "Business is business" and formed her world-combines, collaring monopolies and allowing the individual to survive only by virtue of belonging to the fittest, so now she is saying, "War is war" - something to be accomplished with as little regard to landscapes as blasting a railroad across a continent.

For the first time in the history of this war Germany is "up against" a nation which is going to fight her in her own spirit, borrowing her own methods. This statement needs explaining; its truth was first brought to my attention at American General Headquarters. The French attitude towards the war is utterly personal; it is bayonet to bayonet. It depends on the unflinching courage of every individual French man and woman. The English attitude is that of the knight-errant, seeking high adventures and welcoming death in a noble cause. But the German attitude disregards the individual and knows nothing of gallantry. It lacks utterly the spiritual elation which made the strength of the French at Verdun and of the English at Mons. The German attitude is that of a soulless organisation, invented for one purpose - profitable conquest. War for the Hun is not a final and dreaded atonement for the restoring of justice to the world; it is a business undertaking which, as he is fond of telling us, has never failed to yield him good interest on his capital. I have seen a good deal of the capital he has invested in the battlefields he has lost - men smashed to pulp, bruised by shells out of resemblance to anything human, the breeding place of flies and pestilence, no longer the homes of loyalties and affections. I cannot conceive what percentage of returns can be said to compensate for the agony expended on such indecent Golgothas. However, the Hun has assured us that it pays him; he flatters himself that he is a first-class business man.

But so does the American, and he knows the game from more points of view. For years he has patterned his schools and colleges on German educational methods. What applies to his civilian centres of learning applies to his military as well. German text-books gave the basis for all American military thought. American officers have been trained in German strategy just as thoroughly as if they had lived in Potsdam. At the start of the war many of them were in the field with the German armies as observers. They are able to synchronise their thoughts with the thoughts of their German enemies and at the same time to take advantage of all that the Allies can teach them.

"War is a business," the Germans have said. The Americans, with an ideal shining in their eyes, have replied, "Very well. We didn't want to fight you; but now that you have forced us, we will fight you on your own terms. We will make war on you as a business, for we are businessmen. We will crush you coldly, dispassionately, without rancour, without mercy till we have proved to you that war is not profitable business, but hell."

The American, as I have met him in France, has not changed one iota from the man that he was in New York or Chicago. He has transplanted himself untheatrically to the scenes of battlefields and set himself undisturbedly to the task of dying. There is an amazing normality about him. You find him in towns, ancient with chateaux and wonderful with age; he is absolutely himself, keenly efficient and irreverently modern. Everywhere, from the Bay of Biscay to the Swiss border, from the Mediterranean to the English Channel, you see the lean figure and the slouch hat of the U.S.A. soldier. He is invariably well-conducted, almost always alone and usually gravely absorbed in himself. The excessive gravity of the American in khaki has astonished the men of the other armies who feel that, life being uncertain, it is well to make as genial a use of it as possible while it lasts. The soldier from the U.S.A. seems to stand always restless, alert, alone, listening - waiting for the call to come. He doesn't sink into the landscape the way other troops have done. His impatience picks him out - the impatience of a man in France solely for one purpose. I have seen him thus a thousand times, standing at street-corners, in the crowd but not of it, remarkable to every one but himself. Every man and officer I have spoken to has just one thing to say about what is happening inside him, "Let them take off my khaki and send me back to America, or else hurry me into the trenches. I came here to get started on this job; the waiting makes me tired."

"Let me get into the trenches," that was the cry of the American soldier that I heard on every hand. Having witnessed his eagerness, cleanness and intensity, I ask no more questions as to how he will acquit himself.

I have presented him as an extremely practical person, but no American that I ever met was solely practical. If you watch him closely you will always find that he is doing practical things for an idealistic end. The American who accumulates a fortune to himself, whether it be through corralling railroads, controlling industries, developing mines or establishing a chain of dry-goods stores, doesn't do it for the money only, but because he finds in business the poetry of creating, manipulating, evolving - the exhilaration and adventure of swaying power. And so there came a day when I caught my American soldier dreaming and off his guard.

All day I had been motoring through high uplands. It was a part of France with which I was totally unfamiliar. A thin mist was drifting across the country, getting lost in valleys where it piled up into fleecy mounds, getting caught in tree-tops where it fluttered like tattered banners. Every now and then, with the suddenness of our approach, we would startle an aged shepherd, muffled and pensive as an Arab, strolling slowly across moorlands, followed closely by the sentinel goats which led his flock. The day had been strangely mystic. Time seemed a mood. I had ceased to trouble about where I was going; that

I knew my ultimate destination was sufficient. The way that led to it, which I had never seen before, should never see again perhaps, and through which I travelled at the rate of an express, seemed a fairy non-existent Hollow Land. Landscapes grew blurred with the speed of our passage. They loomed up on us like waves, stayed with us for a second and vanished. The staff-officer, who was my conductor, drowsed on his seat beside the driver. He had wearied himself in the morning, taking me now here to see an American Division putting on a manoeuvre, now there to where the artillery were practising, then to another valley where machine-guns tapped like thousands of busy typewriters working on death's manuscript. After that had come bayonet charges against dummies, rifle-ranges and trench-digging - all the industrious pretence at slaughter which prefaces the astounding actuality. We were far away from all that now; the brown figures had melted into the brownness of the hills. There might have been no war. Perhaps there wasn't. Never was there a world more grey and quiet. I grew sleepy. My head nodded. I opened my eyes, pulled myself together and again nodded. The roar of the engine was soothing. The rush of wind lay heavy against my eye-lids. It seemed odd that I should be here and not in the trenches. When I was in the line I had often made up life's deficiencies by imagining, imagining.... Perhaps I was really in the line now. I wouldn't wake up to find out. That would come presently - it always had.

We were slowing down. I opened my eyes lazily. No, we weren't stopping - only going through a village. What a quaint grey village it was - worth looking at if I wasn't so tired. I was on the point of drowsing off again when I caught sight of a word written on a sign-board, *Domremy*. My brain cleared. I sat up with a jerk. It was magic that I should find myself here without warning - at Domremy, the Bethlehem of warrior-woman's mercy. I had dreamed from boyhood of this place as a legend - a memory of white chivalry to be found on no map, a record of beauty as utterly submerged as the lost land of Lyonesse. Hauntingly the words came back, "Who is this that cometh from Domremy? Who is she in bloody coronation robes from Rheims? Who is she that cometh with blackened flesh from walking in the furnaces of Rouen? This is she, the shepherd girl...." All about me on the little hills were the woodlands through which she must have led her sheep and wandered with her heavenly visions.

We had come to a bend in the village street. Where the road took a turn stood an aged church; nestling beside it in a little garden was a grey, semi-fortified mediaeval dwelling. The garden was surrounded by high spiked railings, planted on a low stone wall. Sitting on the wall beside the entrance was an American soldier. He had a small French child on either knee - one arm about each of them; thus embarrassed he was doing his patient best to roll a Bull Durham cigarette. The children were vividly interested; they laughed up into the soldier's face. One of them was a boy, the other a girl. The long golden curls of the girl brushed against the soldier's cheek. The three heads bent together, almost touching. The scene was timelessly human, despite the modernity of the khaki. Joan of Arc might have been that little girl.

I stopped the driver, got out and approached the group. The soldier jumped to attention and saluted. In answer to my question, he said, "Yes, this is where she lived. That's her house - that grey cottage with scarcely any windows. Bastien le Page could never have seen it; it isn't a bit like his picture in the Metropolitan Gallery."

He spoke in a curiously intimate way as if he had known Joan of Arc and had spoken with her there - as if she had only just departed. It was odd to reflect that America had still lain hidden behind the Atlantic when Joan walked the world.

We entered the gate into the garden, the American soldier, the children and I together. The little girl, with that wistful confidence that all French children show for men in khaki, slipped her grubby little paw into my hand. I expect Joan was often grubby like that.

Brown winter leaves strewed the path. The grass was bleached and dead. At our approach an old sheep-dog rattled his chain and looked out of his kennel. He was shaggy and matted with years. His bark was so weak that it broke in the middle. He was a Rip Van Winkle of a sheep-dog - the kind of dog you would picture in a fairy-tale. One couldn't help feeling that he had accompanied the shepherd girl and had kept the flock from straying while she spoke with her visions. All those centuries ago he had seen her ride away - ride away to save France - and she had not come back. All through the centuries he had waited; at every footstep on the path he had come hopefully out from his kennel, wagging his tail and barking ever more weakly. He would not believe that she was dead. And it was difficult to believe it in that ancient quiet. If ever France needed her, it was now.

Across my memory flashed the words of a dreamer, prophetic in the light of recent events, "Daughter of Domremy, when the gratitude of thy king shall awaken, thou wilt be sleeping the sleep of the dead. Call her, King of France, but she will not hear thee. Cite her by the apparitors to come and receive a robe of honour, but she will not be found. When the thunders of universal France, as even yet may happen, shall proclaim the grandeur of the poor shepherd girl that gave up her all for her country, thy ear, young shepherd girl, will have been deaf five centuries."

Quite illogically it seemed to me that January evening that this American soldier was the symbol of the power that had come in her stead.

The barking of the dog had awakened a bowed old Mother Hubbard lady. She opened the door of her diminutive castle and peered across the threshold, jingling her keys.

Would we come in? Ah, Monsieur from America was there! He was always there when he was not training, playing with the children and rolling cigarettes. And Monsieur, the English officer, perhaps he did not know that she was descended from

Joan's family. Oh, yes, there was no mistake about it; that was why she had been made custodian. She must light the lamp. There! That was better. There was not much to see, but if we would follow....

We stepped down into a flagged room like a cellar - cold, ascetic and bare. There was a big open fire-place, with a chimney hooded by massive masonry and blackened by the fires of immemorial winters. This was where Joan's parents had lived. She had probably been born here. The picture that formed in my mind was not of Joan, but that other woman unknown to history - her mother, who after Joan had left the village and rumours of her battles and banquets drifted back, must have sat there staring into the blazing logs, her peasant's hands folded in her lap, brooding, wondering, hoping, fearing - fearing as the mothers of soldiers have throughout the ages.

And this was Joan's brother's room - a cheerless place of hewn stone. What kind of a man could he have been? What were his reflections as he went about his farm-work and thought of his sister at the head of armies? Was he merely a lout or something worse - the prototype of our Conscientious Objector: a coward who disguised his cowardice with moral scruples?

And this was Joan's room - a cell, with a narrow slit at the end through which one gained a glimpse of the church. Before this slit she had often knelt while the angels drifted from the belfry like doves to peer in on her. The place was sacred. How many nights had she spent here with girlish folded hands, her face ecstatic, the cold eating into her tender body? I see her blue for lack of charity, forgotten, unloved, neglected - the symbol of misunderstanding and loneliness. They told her she was mad. She was a laughing stock in the village. The world could find nothing better for her to do than driving sheep through the bitter woodlands; but God found time to send his angels. Yes, she was mad - mad as Christ was in Galilee - mad enough to save others when she could not save herself. How nearly the sacrifice of this most child-like of women parallels the sacrifice of the most God-like of men! Both were born in a shepherd community; both forewent the humanity of love and parenthood; both gave up their lives that the world might be better; both were royally apparelled in mockery; both followed their visions; for each the price of following was death. She, too, was despised and rejected; as a sheep before her shearers is dumb, so she opened not her mouth.

That is all there is to see at Domremy; three starveling, stone-paved rooms, a crumbling church, a garden full of dead leaves, an old dog growing mangy in his kennel and the wind-swept cathedral of the woodlands. The soul of France was born there in the humble body of a peasant-girl; yes, and more than the soul of France - the gallantry of all womanhood. God must be fond of His peasants; I think they will be His aristocracy in Heaven.

The old lady led us out of the house. There was one more thing she wished to show us. The sunset light was still in the tree-tops, but her eyes were dim; she thought that night had already gathered. Holding her lamp above her head, she pointed to a statue in a niche above the doorway. It had been placed there by order of the King of France after Joan was dead. But it wasn't so much the statue that she wanted us to look at; it was the mutilations that were upon it. She was filled with a great trembling of indignation. "Yes, gaze your fill upon it, Messieurs," she said; "it was _les Boches_ did that. They were here in 1870. To others she may be a saint, but to *them* - Bah!" and she spat, "a woman is less than a woman always."

When we turned to go she was still cursing *les Boches* beneath her breath, tremblingly holding up the lamp above her head that she might forget nothing of their defilement. The old dog rattled his chain as we passed; he knew us now and did not trouble to come out. The dead leaves whispered beneath our tread.

At the gate we halted. I turned to my American soldier. "How long before you go into the line?"

He was carrying the little French girl in his arms. As he glanced up to answer, his face caught the sunset. "Soon now. The sooner, the better. She ...," and I knew he meant no living woman. "This place ... I don't know how to express it. But everything here makes you want to fight, - makes you ashamed of standing idle. If she could do that - well, I guess that I...."

He made no attempt to fill his eloquent silences; and so I left. As the car gathered speed, plunging into the pastoral solitudes, I looked back. The last sight I had of Domremy was a grey little garden, made sacred by the centuries, and an American soldier standing with a French child in his arms, her golden hair lying thickly against his neck.

On the surface the American is unemotionally practical, but at heart he is a dreamer, first, last and always. If the Americans have merited any criticism in France, it is owing to the vastness of their plans; the tremendous dream of their preparations postpones the beginning of the reality. Their mistake, if they have made a mistake, is an error of generosity. They are building with a view to flinging millions into the line when thousands a little earlier would be of superlative advantage. They had the choice of dribbling their men over in small contingents or of waiting till they could put a fighting-force into the field so overwhelming in equipment and numbers that its weight would be decisive. They were urged to learn wisdom from England's example and not to waste their strength by putting men into the trenches in a hurry before they were properly trained. England was compelled to adopt this chivalrous folly by the crying need of France. It looked in the Spring of 1917, before Russia had broken down or the pressure on the Italian front had become so menacing, as though the Allies could afford to ask America to conduct her war on the lines of big business. America jumped at the chance - big business being the task to which her national genius was best suited. If her Allies could hold on long enough, she would build her fleet and appear with an army of millions that would bring the war to a rapid end. Her role was to be that of the toreador in the European bull-fight.

But big business takes time and usually loses money at the start. In the light of recent developments, we would rather have the bird-in-the-hand of 300,000 Americans actually fighting than the promise of a host a year from now. People at home in America realised this in January. They were so afraid that their Allies might feel disappointed. They were so keen to achieve tangible results in the war that they grew impatient with the long delay. They weren't interested in seeing other nations going over the top - the same nations who had been over so many times; they wanted to see their sons and brothers at once given the opportunity to share the wounds and the danger. Their attitude was Spartan and splendid; they demanded a curtailment of their respite that they might find themselves afloat on the crimson tide. The cry of the civilians in America was identical with that of their men in France. "Let them take off our khaki or else hurry us into the trenches. We want to get started. This waiting makes us tired."

And the civilians in America had earned a right to make their demand. Industrially, financially, philanthropically, from every point of view they had sacrificed and played the game, both by the Allies and their army. When they, as civilians, had been so willing to wear the stigmata of sacrifice, they were jealous lest their fighting men should be baulked of their chance of making those sacrifices appear worth while.

There have been many accusations in the States with regard to the supposed breakdown of their military organization in France - accusations inspired by generosity towards the Allies. From what I have seen, and I have been given liberal opportunities to see everything, I do not think that those accusations are justified. As a combatant of another nation, I have my standards of comparison by which to judge and I frankly state that I was amazed with the progress that had been made. It is a progress based on a huge scale and therefore less impressive to the layman than if the scale had been less ambitious. What I saw were the foundations of an organisation which can be expanded to handle a fighting-machine which staggers the imagination. What the layman expects to see are

Hun trophies and Americans coming out of the line on stretchers. He will see all that, if he waits long enough, for the American military hospitals in France are being erected to accommodate 200,000 wounded.

Unfounded optimisms, which under no possible circumstances could ever have been realised, are responsible for the disappointment felt in America. Inasmuch as these optimisms were widely accepted in England and France, civilian America's disappointment will be shared by the Allies, unless some hint of the truth is told as to what may be expected and what great preparations are under construction. It was generally believed that by the spring of 1918 America would have half a million men in the trenches and as many more behind the lines, training to become reinforcements. People who spoke this way could never have seen a hundred thousand men or have stopped to consider what transport would be required to maintain them at a distance of more than three thousand miles from their base. It was also believed that by the April of 1918, one year after the declaring of war, America would have manufactured ten thousand planes, standardised all their parts, trained the requisite number of observers and pilots, and would have them flying over the Hun lines. Such beliefs were pure moonshine, incapable of accomplishment; but there are facts to be told which are highly honourable.

So far I have tried to give a glimpse of America's fighting spirit in facing up to her job; now, in as far as it is allowed, I want to give a sketch of her supreme earnestness as proved by what she has already achieved in France. The earnestness of her civilians should require no further proof than the readiness with which they accepted national conscription within a few hours of entering the war - a revolutionising departure which it took England two years of fighting even to contemplate, and which can hardly be said to be in full operation yet, so long as conscientious objectors are allowed to air their so-called consciences. In America the conscientious objector is not regarded; he is listened to as only one of two things - a deserter or a traitor. The earnestness of America's fighting man requires no proving; his only grievance is that he is not in the trenches. Yet so long as the weight of America is not felt to be turning the balance dramatically in our favour, the earnestness of America will be open to challenge both by Americans and by the Allies. What I saw in France in the early months of this year has filled me with unbounded optimism. I feel the elated certainty, as never before even in the moment of the most successful attack, that the Hun's fate is sealed. What is more, I have grounds for believing that he knows it - knows that the collapse of Russia will profit him nothing because he cannot withstand the avalanche of men from America. Already he hears them, as I have seen them, training in their camps from the Pacific to the Atlantic, racing across the Ocean in their grey transports, marching along the dusty roads of two continents, a procession locust-like in multitude, stretching half about the world, marching and singing indomitably, "We've got four years to do this job." From behind the Rhine he has caught their singing; it grows ever nearer, stronger. It will take time for that avalanche to pyramid on the Western Front; but when it has piled up, it will rush forward, fall on him and crush him. He knows something else, which fills him with a still more dire sense of calamity - that because America's honour has been jeopardised, of all the nations now fighting she will be the last to lay down her arms. She has given herself four years to do her job; when her job is ended, it will be with Prussianism as it was with Jezebel, "They that went to bury her found no more of her than the skull and the feet and the palms of her hands. And her carcase was as dung upon the face of the field, so that men should not say, 'This is Jezebel.'"

As an example of what America is accomplishing, I will take a sample port in France. It was of tenth-rate importance, little more than a harbour for coastwise vessels and ocean-going tramps when the Americans took it over; by the time they have finished, it will be among the first ports of Europe. It is only one of several that they are at present enlarging and constructing. The work already completed has been done in the main under the direction of the engineers who marched through London in the July of last year. I visited the port in

January, so some idea can be gained of how much has been achieved in a handful of months.

The original French town still has the aspect of a prosperous fishing-village. There are two main streets with shops on them; there is one out-of-date hotel; there are a few modern dwellings facing the sea. For the rest, the town consists of cottages, alleys and open spaces where the nets were once spread to dry. To-day in a vast circle, as far as eye can reach, a city of huts has grown up. In those huts live men of many nations, Americans, French, German prisoners, negroes. They are all engaged in the stupendous task of construction. The capacity of the harbour basin is being multiplied fifty times, the berthing capacity trebled, the unloading facilities multiplied by ten. A railroad yard is being laid which will contain 225 miles of track and 870 switches. An immense locomotive-works is being erected for the repairing and assembling of rolling-stock from America. It was originally planned to bring over 960 standard locomotives and 30,000 freight-cars from the States, all equipped with French couplers and brakes so that they could become a permanent part of the French railroad system. These figures have since been somewhat reduced by the purchase of rolling-stock in Europe. Reservoirs are being built at some distance from the town which will be able to supply six millions gallons of purified water a day. In order to obtain the necessary quantity of pipe, piping will be torn up from various of the water-systems in America and brought across the Atlantic. As the officer, who was my informant remarked, "Rather than see France go short, some city in the States will have to haul water in carts."

As proof of the efficiency with which materials from America are being furnished, when the engineers arrived on the scene with 225 miles of track to lay, they found 100 miles of rails and spikes already waiting for them. Of the 870 switches required, 350 were already on hand. Of the ties required, one-sixth were piled up for them to be going on with. Not so bad for a nation quite new to the war-game and living three thousand miles beyond the horizon!

On further enquiry I learnt that six million cubic yards of filling were necessary to raise the ground of the railroad yard to the proper level. In order that the work may be hurried, dredges are being brought across the Atlantic and, if necessary, harbour construction in the States will be curtailed.

I was interested in the personnel employed in this work. Here, as elsewhere, I found that the engineering and organising brains of America are largely in France. One colonel was head of the marble industry in the States; another had been vice-president of the Pennsylvania Railroad. Another man, holding a sergeant's rank was general manager of the biggest fishing company. Another, a private in the ranks, was chief engineer of the American Aluminum Company. A major was general manager of The Southern Pacific. Another colonel was formerly controller of the currency and afterwards president of the Central Trust Company of Illinois. A captain was chief engineer and built the aqueducts over the keys of the Florida East Coast Railroad. As with us, you found men of the highest social and professional grade serving in every rank of the American Army; one, a society man and banker, was running a gang of negroes whose job it was to shovel sand into cars. In peace times thirty thousand pounds a year could not have bought him. What impressed me even more than the line of communications itself was the quality of the men engaged on its construction. As one of them said to me, "Any job that they give us engineers to do over here is likely to be small in comparison with the ones we've had to tackle in America." The man who said this had previously done his share in the building of the Panama Canal. There were others I met, men who had spanned rivers in Alaska, flung rails across the Rockies, built dams in the arid regions, performed engineering feats in China, Africa, Russia - in all parts of the world. They were trained to be undaunted by the hugeness of any task; they'd always beaten Nature in the long run. Their cheerful certainty that America in France was more than up to her job maintained a constant wave of enthusiasm.

It may be asked why it is necessary in an old-established

country like France, to waste time in enlarging harbours before you can make effective war. The answer is simple: France has not enough ports of sufficient size to handle the tonnage that is necessary to support the Allied armies within her borders. America's greatest problem is tonnage. She has the men and the materials in prodigal quantities, but they are all three thousand miles away. Before the men can be brought over, she has to establish her means of transport and line of communications, so as to make certain that she can feed and clothe them when once she has got them into the front-line. There are two ways of economising on tonnage. One is to purchase in Europe. In this way, up to February, The Purchasing Board of the Americans had saved ninety days of transatlantic traffic. The other way is to have modern docks, well railroaded, so that vessels can be unloaded in the least possible space of time and sent back for other cargoes. Hence it has been sane economy on the part of America to put much of her early energy into construction rather than into fighting. Nevertheless, it has made her an easy butt for criticism both in the States and abroad, since the only proof to the newspaper-reader that America is at war is the amount of front-line that she is actually defending.

I had heard much of what was going on at a certain place which was to be the intermediate point in the American line of communications. I had studied a blue-print map and had been amazed at its proportions. I was told, and can well believe, that when completed it was to be the biggest undertaking of its kind in the world. It was to be six and a half miles long by about one mile broad. It was to have four and a half million feet of covered storage and ten million feet of open storage. It was to contain over two hundred miles of track in its railroad yard and to house enough of the materials of war to keep a million men fully equipped for thirty days. In addition to this it was to have a plant, not for the repairing, but merely for the assembling of aeroplanes, which would employ twenty thousand men.

I arrived there at night. There was no town. One stepped from the train into the open country. Far away in the distance there was a glimmering of fires and the scarlet of sparks shooting up between bare tree-tops. My first impression was of the fragrance of pines and, after that, as I approached the huts, of a memory more definite and elusively familiar. The swinging of lanterns helped to bring it back: I was remembering lumber-camps in the Rocky Mountains. The box-stove in the shack in which I slept that night and the roughly timbered walls served to heighten the illusion that I was in America. Next morning the illusion was completed. Here were men with mackinaws and green elk boots; here were cook-houses in which the only difference was that a soldier did the cooking instead of a Chinaman; and above all, here were fir and pines growing out of a golden soil, with a soft wind blowing overhead. And here, in an extraordinary way, the democracy of a lumber-camp had been reproduced: every one from the Colonel down was a worker; it was difficult, apart from their efficiency, to tell their rank.

Early in the morning I started out on a gasolene-speeder to make the tour. At an astonishing rate, for the work had only been in hand three months, the vast acreage was being tracked and covered with the sheds. The sheds were not the kind I had been used to on my own front; they were built out of anything that came handy, commenced with one sort of material and finished with another. Sometimes the cross-pieces in the roofs were still sweating, proving that it was only yesterday they had been cut down in the nearby wood. There was no look of permanence about anything. As the officer who conducted me said, "It's all run up - a race against time." And then he added with a twinkle in his eye, "But it's good enough to last four years."

This was America in France in every sense of the word. One felt the atmosphere of rush. In the buildings, which should have been left when materials failed, but which had been carried to completion by pioneer methods, one recognised the resourcefulness of the lumberman of the West. Then came a touch of Eastern America, to me almost more replete with memory and excitement. In a flash I was transferred from a camp in France to the rock-hewn highway of Fifth Avenue, running through groves of sky-scrapers, garnished with sunshine and echoing with tripping footsteps. I could smell the asphalt soaked with gasolene and the flowers worn by the passing girls. The whole movement and quickness of the life I had lost flooded back on me. The sound I heard was the fate *motif* of the frantic opera of American endeavour. The truly wonderful thing was that I should hear it here, in a woodland in France - the rapid tapping of a steel-riveter at work.

I learnt afterwards that I was not the only one to be carried away by that music, as of a monstrous wood-pecker in an iron forest. The first day the riveter was employed, the whole camp made excuses to come and listen to it. They stood round it in groups, deafened and thrilled - and a little homesick. What the bag-pipe is to the Scotchman, the steel-riveter is to the American - the instrument which best expresses his soul to a world which is different.

I found that the riveter was being employed in the erection of an immense steel and concrete refrigerating plant, which was to have machinery for the production of its own ice and sufficient meat-storage capacity to provide a million men for thirty days. The water for the ice was being obtained from wells which had been already sunk. There was only surface water there when the Americans first struck camp.

As another clear-cut example of what America is accomplishing in France, I will take an aviation-camp. This camp is one of several, yet it alone will be turning out from 350 to 400 airmen a month. The area which it covers runs into miles. The Americans have their own ideas of aerial fighting tactics, which they will teach here on an intensive course and try out on the Hun from time to time. Some of their experts have had the advantage of familiarising themselves with Hun aerial equipment and strategy; they were on his side of the line at the start of the war as neutral military observers. I liked the officer at the head of this camp; I was particularly pleased with some of his phrases. He was one of the first experts to fly with a Liberty engine. Without giving any details away, he assured me impressively that it was "an honest-to-God engine" and that his planes were equipped with "an honest-to-God machine-gun," and that he looked forward with cheery anticipation to the first encounter his chaps would have with "the festive Hun." He was one of the few Americans I had met who spoke with something of our scornful affection for the enemy. It indicated to me his absolute certainty that he could beat him at the flying game. On his lips the Hun was never the German or the Boche, but always "the festive Hun." You can afford to speak kindly, almost pityingly of some one you are going to vanquish. Hatred often indicates fear. Jocularity is a victorious sign.

When I was in America last October a great effort was being made to produce an overwhelming quantity of aeroplanes. Factories, both large and small, in every State were specializing on manufacturing certain parts, the idea being that so time would be saved and efficiency gained. These separate parts were to be collected and assembled at various big government plants. The aim was to turn out planes as rapidly as Ford Cars and to swamp the Hun with numbers. America is unusually rich in the human as well as the mechanical material for crushing the enemy in the air. In this service, as in all the others, the only difficulty that prevents her from making her fighting strength immediately felt is the difficulty of transportation. The road of ships across the Atlantic has to be widened; the road of steel from the French ports to the Front has to be tracked and multiplied in its carrying capacity. These difficulties on land and water are being rapidly overcome: by adding to the means of transportation; by increasing the efficiency of the transport facilities already existing; by lightening the tonnage to be shipped from the States by buying everything that is procurable in Europe. In the early months much of the available Atlantic tonnage was occupied with carrying the materials of construction: rails, engines, concrete, lumber, and all the thousand and one things that go to the housing of armies. This accounts for America's delay in starting fighting. For three years Europe had been ransacked; very much of what America would require had to be brought. Such work does not make a dramatic impression on other nations, especially when they are impatient. Its value as a contribution towards defeating the Hun is all in the future. Only victories win applause in these days. Nevertheless, such work had to be done. To do it thoroughly, on a sufficiently large scale, in the face of the certain criticism which the delay for thoroughness would occasion, demanded bravery and patriotism on the part of those in charge of affairs. By the time this book is published their high-mindedness will have begun to be appreciated, for the results of it will have begun to tell. The results will tell increasingly as the war progresses. America is determined to have no Crimea scandals. The contentment and good condition of her troops in France will be largely owing to the organisation and care with which her line of communications has been constructed.

The purely business side of war is very dimly comprehended either by the civilian or the combatant. The combatant, since he does whatever dying is to be done, naturally looks down on the business man in khaki. The civilian is inclined to think of war in terms of the mobile warfare of other days, when armies were rarely more than some odd thousands strong and were usually no more than expeditionary forces. Such armies by reason of their rapid movements and the comparative fewness of their numbers, were able to live on the countries through which they marched. But our fighting forces of to-day are the manhood of nations. The fronts which they occupy can scarcely boast a blade of grass. The towns which lie behind them have been picked clean to the very marrow. France herself, into which a military population of many millions has been poured, was never at the best of times entirely self-supporting. Whatever surplus of commodities the Allies possessed, they had already shared long before the spring of 1917. When America landed into the war, she found herself in the position of one who arrives at an overcrowded inn late at night. Whatever of food or accommodation the inn could afford had been already apportioned; consequently, before

America could put her first million men into the trenches, she had to graft on to France a piece of the living tissue of her own industrial system - whole cities of repair-shops, hospitals, dwellings, store-houses, ice-plants, etc., together with the purely business personnel that go with them. These cities, though initially planned to maintain and furnish a minimum number of fighting men, had to be capable of expansion so that they could ultimately support millions.

Here are some facts and statistics which illustrate the big business of war as Americans have undertaken it. They have had to erect cold storage-plants, with mechanical means for ice-manufacture, of sufficient capacity to hold twenty-five million pounds of beef always in readiness.

They are at present constructing two salvage depots which, when completed, will be the largest in the world. Here they will repair and make fit for service again, shoes, harness, clothing, webbing, tentage, rubber-boots, etc. Attached to these buildings there are to be immense laundries which will undertake the washing for all the American forces. In connection with the depots, there will be a Salvage Corps, whose work is largely at the Front. The materials which they collect will be sent back to the depots for sorting. Under the American system every soldier, on coming out of the trenches, will receive a complete new outfit, from the soles of his feet to the crown of his head. "This," the General who informed me said tersely, "is our way of solving the lice-problem."

The Motor Transport also has its salvage depot. Knock-down buildings and machinery have been brought over from the States, and upwards of 4,000 trained mechanics for a start. This depot is also responsible for the repairs of all horse-drawn transport, except the artillery. The Quartermaster General's Department alone will have 35,000 motor propelled vehicles and a personnel of 160,000 men.

Every effort is being made to employ labour-saving devices to the fullest extent. The Supply Department expects to cut down its personnel by two-thirds through the efficient use of machinery and derricks. The order compelling all packages to be standardized in different graded sizes, so that they can be forwarded directly to the Front before being broken, has already done much to expedite transportation. The dimensions of the luggage of a modern army can be dimly realized when it is stated that the American armies will initially require twenty-four million square feet of covered and forty-one million of unroofed storage - not to mention the barrack space.

Within the next few months they will require bakeries capable of feeding one million and a quarter men. These bakeries are divided into: the field bakeries, which are portable, and the mechanical bakeries which are stationary and on the line of communications. One of the latter had just been acquired and was described to me when I was in the American area. It was planned throughout with a view to labour-saving. It was so constructed that it could take the flour off the cars and, with practically no handling, convert it into bread at the rate of 750,000 lbs. a day. This struck me as a peculiarly American contribution to big business methods; but on expressing this opinion I was immediately corrected. This form of bakery was a British invention, which has been in use for some time on our lines. The Americans owed their possession of the bakery to the courtesy of the British Government, who had postponed their own order and allowed the Americans to fill theirs four months ahead of their contract.

This is a sample of the kind of discovery that I was perpetually making. Two out of three times when I thought I had run across a characteristically American expression of efficiency, I was told that it had been copied from the British. I learnt more about my own army's business efficiency in studying it secondhand with the Americans, than I had ever guessed existed in all the time that I had been an inhabitant of the British Front. It is characteristic of us as a people that we like to pretend that we muddle our way into success. We advertise our mistakes and camouflage our virtues. We are almost ashamed of gaining credit for anything that we have done well.

There is a fine dishonesty about this self-belittlement; but it is not always wise. During these first few months of their being at war the Americans have discovered England in almost as novel a sense as Columbus did America. It was a joy to be with them and to watch their surprise. The odd thing was that they had had to go to France to find us out. Here they were, the picked business men of the world's greatest industrial nation, frankly and admiringly hats off to British "muddle-headed" methods. Not only were they hats off to the methods, many of which they were copying, but they were also hats off to the generous helpfulness of our Government and Military authorities in the matter of advice, co-operation and supplies. From the private in the ranks, who had been trained by British N.C.O.'s and Officers, to the Generals at the head of departments, there was only one feeling expressed for Great Britain - that of a new sincerity of friendship and admiration. "John Bull and his brother Jonathan" had become more than an empty phrase; it expressed a true and living relation.

A similar spirit of appreciation had grown up towards the French - not the emotional, histrionic, Lafayette appreciation with which the American troops sailed from America, but an appreciation based on sympathy and a knowledge of deeds and character. I think this spirit was best illustrated at Christmas when all over France, wherever American troops were billeted, the rank and file put their hands deep into their pockets to give the refugee children of their district the first real Christmas they had had since their country was invaded. Officers were selected to go to Paris to do the purchasing of the presents, and I know of at least one case in which the men's gift was so generous that there was enough money left over to provide for the children throughout the coming year.

In France one hears none of that patronising criticism which used to exist in America with regard to the older nations - none of those arrogant assertions that "because we are younger we can do things better." The bias of the American in France is all the other way; he is near enough to the Judgment Day, which he is shortly to experience, to be reverent in the presence of those who have stood its test. He is in France to learn as well as to contribute. Between himself and his brother soldiers of the British and French armies, there exists an entirely manly and reciprocal respect. And it is reciprocal; both the individual British and French fighting-man, now that they have seen the American soldier, are clamorous to have him adjacent to their line. The American has scarcely been blooded at this moment, and yet, having seen him, they are both certain that he's not the pal to let them down.

The confidence that the American soldier has created among his soldier-Allies was best expressed to me by a British officer: "The British, French and Americans are the three great promise-keeping nations. For the first time in history we're standing together. We're promise-keepers banded together against the falsehood of Germany - that's why. It isn't likely that we shall start to tell lies to one another."

Not likely!

Coningsby Dawson

III

THE WAR OF COMPASSION

Officially America declared war on Germany in the spring of 1917; actually she committed her heart to the allied cause in September, 1914, when the first shipment of the supplies of mercy arrived in Paris from the American Red Cross.

There are two ways of waging war: you can fight with artillery and armed men; you can fight with ambulances and bandages. There's the war of destruction and the war of compassion. The one defeats the enemy directly with force; the other defeats him indirectly by maintaining the morale of the men who are fighting and, what is equally important, of the civilians behind the lines. Belgium would not be the utterly defiant and unconquered nation that she is to-day, had it not been for the mercy of Hoover and his disciples. Their voluntary presence made the captured Belgian feel that he was earning the thanks of all time - that the eyes of the world were upon him. They were neutrals, but their mere presence condemned the cause that had brought them there. Their compassion waged war against the Hun. The same is true of the American Ambulance Units which followed the French Armies into the fiercest of the carnage. They confirmed the poilu in his burning sense of injustice. That they, who could have absented themselves, should choose the damnation of destruction and dare the danger, convinced the entire French nation of its own righteousness. And it was true of the girls at the American hospitals who nursed the broken bodies which their brothers had rescued. It was true of Miss Holt's *Lighthouse* for the training of blinded soldiers, which she established in Paris within eight months of war's commencement. It was true of the American Relief Clearing House in Paris which, up to January, 1917, had received 291 shipments and had distributed eight million francs. By the time America put on armour, the American Red Cross, as the army's expert in the strategy of compassion, found that it had to take over more than eighty-six separate organisations which had been operating in France for the best part of two years.

One cannot show pity with indignant hands and keep the mind neutral. The Galilean test holds true, "He who is not for me is against me." You cannot leave houses, lands, children, wife - everything that counts - for the Kingdom of Heaven's sake without developing a rudimentary aversion for the devil. All of which goes to prove that America's heart was fighting for the Allies long before her ambassador requested his passports from the Kaiser.

The American Red Cross Commission landed in France on the 12th of June, 1917, seven days ahead of the Expeditionary Force. It had taken less than five days to organise. Its first act was to convey a monetary gift to the French hospitals. The first actual American Red Cross contribution was made in April to the Number Five British Base Hospital. The first American soldiers in France were doctors and nurses. The first American fighting done in France was done with the weapons of pity. The chief function of the American Red Cross up to the present has been to "carry on" and to bridge the gap of unavoidable delays while the army is preparing.

To prove that this "war of compassion" is no idle phrase, let me illustrate with one dramatic instance. When the Italian line broke under the pressure of Hun artillery and propaganda, the American Red Cross sent representatives forward to inaugurate relief work for the 700,000 refugees, who were pouring southward from the Friuti and Veneto, homeless, hungry, possessing nothing but misfortune, spreading despair and panic every step of the journey. Their bodies must be cared for - that was evident; it would be easy for them to carry disease throughout Italy. But the disease of their minds was an even greater danger; if their demoralisation were not checked, it would inevitably prove contagious.

The first two representatives of the American Red Cross arrived in Rome on November 5th, with a quarter of a million dollars at their disposal. That night they had a soup-kitchen going and fed 400 people. Their first day's work is the record of an amazing spurt of energy. In that first day they sent money for relief to every American Consul in the districts affected. They mobilised the American colony in Rome and arranged by wire for similar organisations to be formed throughout the length and breadth of Italy, wherever they could lay hands on an American. On all principal junction points through which the refugees would pass, soup-kitchens were installed and clothes were purchased and ready to be distributed as the trains pulled into the stations. They were badly needed, for the passengers had endured all the rigours of the retreat with the soldiers. They had been under shell and machine-gun fire. They had been bombed by aeroplanes. No horror of warfare had been spared them. Their clothes were verminous with weeks of wearing. They were packed like cattle. Babies born on the journey were wrapped in newspapers. There were instances of officers taking off their shirts that the little bodies should not go naked. A telegram was at once despatched to Paris for food and clothes and hospital supplies. Twenty-four cars came through within a week, despite the unusual military traffic. This ends the list of what was accomplished by two men in one day.

The great thing was to make the demoralised Italians feel that America was on the spot and helping them. The sending of troops could not have reused their fighting spirit. They were sick of fighting. What they needed was the assurance that the world was not wholly brutal - that there was some one who was merciful, who did not condemn and who was moved by their sorrow. This assurance the prompt action of the

American Red Cross gave. It restored in the affirmative with mercy, precisely the quality which Hun fury and propaganda had destroyed with lies. It restored to them their belief in the nobility of mankind, out of which belief grows all true courage.

As the work progressed, it branched out on a much larger scale, embracing civilian, military and child-welfare activities. In the month of November upward of half a million lire were placed in the hands of American consuls for distribution. One million lire were contributed for the benefit of soldiers' families. A permanent headquarters was established with trained business men and men who had had experience under Hoover in Belgium in charge of its departments. Over 100 hospitals and two principal magazines of hospital stores had been lost in the retreat. The American Red Cross made up this deficiency by supplying the bedding for no less than 3,000 beds. Five weeks after the first two representatives had reached Rome three complete ambulance sections, each section being made up of 20 ambulances, a staff car, a kitchen trailer and 33 men, were turned over to the Italian Medical Service of the third Army. By the first week in December the stream of refugees had practically stopped. Italy had been made to realise that she was not fighting alone; her morale had returned to her. This work, which had been initially undertaken from purely altruistic motives, had proved to possess a value of the highest military importance - an importance of the spirit utterly out of proportion to the money and labour expended. Magnanimity arouses magnanimity. In this case it revived the flame of Garibaldi which had all but died. It achieved a strategic victory of the soul which no amount of military assistance could have accomplished. The victory of the American Red Cross on the Italian Front is all the more significant since it was not until months later that Congress declared war on Austria.

The campaign which the American Red Cross is waging in every country in which it operates, is frankly an "out to win" campaign. To win the war is its one and only object. What the army does for the courage of the body, the Red Cross does for the courage of the mind. It builds up the hearts and hopes of people who in three and a half years have grown numb. It restores the human touch to their lives and, with it, the spiritual horizon. Its business, while the army is still preparing, is to bring home to the Allies in every possible way the fact that America, with her hundred and ten millions of population, is in the war with them, eager to play the game, anxious to sacrifice as they have sacrificed, to give her man-power and resources as they have done, until justice has been established for every man and nation.

It is necessary to lay stress on this programme since it differs greatly from the popular conception of the functions of the Red Cross in the battle area. It was on the field of Solferino in 1859, that Henri Dunant went out before the fury had spent itself to tend the wounded. It was here that he was fired with his great ambition to found a non-combatant service, which should recognise no enemies and be friends with every army. His ambition was realised when in 1864 the Conference at Geneva chose the Swiss flag, reversed, as its emblem - a red cross on a field of white - and laid the foundations for those international understandings which have since formed for all combatants, except the Hun in this present warfare, the protective law for the sick and wounded. The original purpose of the Red Cross still fills the imagination of the masses to the exclusion of all else that it is doing. Directly the term "Red Cross" is mentioned the picture that forms in most men's minds is of ambulances galloping through the thick of battle-smoke and of devoted stretcher-bearers who brave danger not to kill, but in order that they may save lives.

This war has changed all that. To-day the Red Cross has to minister to not the wounded of armies only, but to the wounded of nations. In a country like France, with trenches dug the entire length of her eastern frontier and vast territories from which the entire population has been evacuated, the wounds of her armies are small in comparison with the wounds, bodily and mental, of her civil population - wounds which are the outcome of over three years of privation. When the civil population of any country has lost its pluck, no matter how splendid the spirit of its soldiers, its armies become paralysed. The civilians can commence peace negotiations behind the backs of their men in the trenches. They can insist on peace by refusing to send them ammunition and supplies. As a matter of fact the morale of the soldiers varies directly with the morale of the civilians for whom they fight. Behind every soldier stand a woman and a group of children. Their safety is his inspiration. If they are neglected, his sacrifice is belittled. If they beg that he should lay down his arms, his determination is weakened. It is therefore a vital necessity, quite apart from the humanitarian aspect, that the wounds of the civilians of belligerent countries should be cared for. If the civilians are allowed to become disheartened and cowardly, the heroic ideal of their fighting-men is jeopardised. This fact has been recognised by the Red Cross Societies of all countries in the present war; a large part of their energies has been devoted to social and relief work of a civil nature. Even in their purely military departments, the comfort of the troops claims quite as much attention as their medical treatment and hospitalisation. As a matter of fact, the actual carrying of the wounded out of the trenches to the comparative safety of the dressing station is usually done by combatants. A man has to live continually under shell-fire to acquire the immunity to fear which passes for courage. The bravest man is likely to get "jumpy," if he only faces up to a bombardment occasionally. There are other reasons why combatants should do the stretcher-bearing which do not need elaborating. The combatants have an expert knowledge of their own particular frontage; they are "wise" to the barraged areas; they are "up front" and continually coming and going, so it is often an economy of man-power for them to attend to their own wounded in the initial stages; they are the nearest to a comrade when he falls and all carry the necessary first-aid dressings; the emblem of the Red Cross has proved to be only a slight protection, as the Hun is quite likely not to respect it. What I am driving at is that the Red Cross has had to adapt itself to the new conditions of modern warfare, so that very many of its most important present-day functions are totally different from what popular fancy imagines.

The American Red Cross has its French Headquarters in a famous gambling club in the Place de la Concorde. It is somewhat strange to pass through these rooms where rakes once flung away fortunes, and to find them industriously orderly with the conscience of an imported nation. By far the larger part of the staff are business men of the Wall Street type - not at all the kind who have been accustomed to sentimentalise over philanthropy. There is also a sprinkling of trained social workers, clergy, journalists, and university professors. The medical profession is represented by some of the leading specialists of the States, but at Headquarters they are distinctly in the minority. The purely medical work of the American Red Cross forms only a part of its total activities. The men at the head of affairs are bankers, merchants, presidents of corporations - men who have been trained to think in millions and to visualise broad areas. Girls are very much in evidence. They are usually volunteers, drawn from all classes, who offered their services to do anything that would help. To-day they are typists, secretaries, stenographers, nurses.

The organisation is divided into three main departments: the department of military affairs, of civil affairs and of administration. Under these departments come a variety of bureaus: the bureau of rehabilitation and reconstruction; of the care and prevention of tuberculosis; of needy children and infant mortality; of refugees and relief; of the re-education of the French mutiles; of supplies; of the rolling canteens for the French armies; of the U.S. Army Division; of the Military, Medical and Surgical Division, etc. They are too numerous to mention in detail. The best way I can convey the picture of immense accomplishment is to describe what I actually saw in the field of operations.

The first place I will take you to is Evian, because here you see the tragedy and need of France as embodied in individuals. Evian-les-Bains is on Lake Geneva, looking out across the water to Switzerland. It is the first point of call across the

French frontier for the repatries returning from their German bondage. When the Boche first swept down on the northern provinces he pushed the French civilian population behind him. He has since kept them working for him as serfs, labouring in the captured coal-mines, digging his various lines of defences, setting up wire-entanglements, etc. Apart from the testimony of repatriated French civilians, I myself have seen messages addressed by Frenchmen to their wives, scrawled surreptitiously on the planks of Hun dug-outs in the hope that one day the dug-outs would be captured, and the messages passed on by a soldier of the Allies. After three and a half years of enforced labour, many of these captured civilians are worked out. To the Boche, with his ever-increasing food-shortage, they represent useless mouths. Instead of filling them he is driving their owners back, broken and useless, by way of Switzerland. To him human beings are merchandise to be sold upon the hoof like cattle. No spiritual values enter into the bargain. When the body is exhausted it is sent to the knacker's, as though it belonged to a worn-out horse. The entire attitude is materialistic and degrading. Evian-les-Bains, the once gay gambling resort of the cosmopolitan, has become the knacker's shop for French civilians exhausted by their German servitude. The Hun shoves them across the border at the rate of about 1,300 a day. From the start I have always felt that this war was a crusade; what I saw at Evian made me additionally certain. When I was in the trenches I never had any hatred of the Boche. Probably I shall lose my hatred in pity for him when I get to the Front again - but for the present I hate him. It's here in France that one sees what a vileness he has created in the children's and women's lives.

I took the night train down from Paris. Early in the morning I woke up to find myself in the gorges of the Alps, high peaks with romantic Italian-looking settings soaring on every side. At noon we reached Lake Geneva, lying slate-coloured and sombre beneath a wintry sky. That afternoon I saw the train of repatries arrive.

I was on the platform when the train pulled into the station. It might have been a funeral cortege, only there was a horrible difference: the corpses pretended to be alive. The American Ambulance men were there in force. They climbed into the carriages and commenced to help the infirm to alight. The exiles were all so stiff with travel that they could scarcely move at first. The windows of the train were grey with faces. Such faces! All of them old, even the little children's. The Boche makes a present to France of only such human wreckage as is unuseful for his purposes. He is an acute man of business. The convoy consisted of two classes of persons - the very ancient and the very juvenile. You can't set a man of eighty to dig trenches and you can't make a prostitute out of a girl-child of ten. The only boys were of the mal-nourished variety. Men, women and children - they all had the appearance of being half-witted.

They were terribly pathetic. As I watched them I tried to picture to myself what three and a half long years of captivity must have meant. How often they must have dreamt of the exaltation of this day - and now that it had arrived, they were not exalted. They had the look of people so spiritually benumbed that they would never know despair or exaltation again. They had a broken look; their shoulders were crushed and their skirts bedraggled. Many of them carried babies - pretty little beggars with flaxen hair. It wasn't difficult to guess their parentage.

As they were herded on the platform a low, strangled kind of moaning went up. I watched individual lips to see where the sound came from. I caught no movement. The noise was the sighing of tired animals. Every one had some treasured possession. Here was an old man with an alarm-clock; there an aged woman with an empty bird-cage. A boy carried half-a-dozen sauce-pans strung together. Another had a spare pair of patched boots under his arm. Quite a lot of them clutched a bundle of umbrellas. I found myself reflecting that these were the remnants of families who had been robbed of everything that they valued in the world. Whatever they had saved from the ruin ought to represent the possession which had claimed most of their affections, and yet - ! What did an alarm-clock, an empty bird-cage, a pair of patched boots, a string of sauce-pans, a bundle of ragged umbrellas signify in any life? What utter poverty, if these were the best that they could save!

There was a band on the platform, consisting mainly of bugles and drums, to welcome them. The leader is reputed to be the laziest man in the French Army. It is said that they tried him at everything and then, in despair, sent him to Evian to drum forgotten happiness into the bones of repatries. Whatever his former military record, he now does his utmost to impersonate the defiant and impassioned soul of France. His moustaches are curled fiercely. His brows are heavy as thunderclouds. When he drums, the veins swell out in his neck with the violence of his energy.

Suddenly, with an ominous preliminary rumble, the band struck up the Marseillaise. You should have seen the change in this crowd of corpses. You must remember that these people had been so long accustomed to lies and snares that it would probably take days to persuade them that they were actually safe home in France.

As the battle-song for which they had suffered shook the air their lips rustled like leaves. There was hardly any sound - only a hoarse whisper. Then, all of a sudden, words came - an inarticulate, sobbing commotion. Tears blinded the eyes of every spectator, even those who had witnessed similar scenes often; we were crying because the singing was so little human.

"Vive la France! Vive la France!" They waved flags - not the tri-colour, but flags which had been given them in Switzerland. They clung together dazed, women with slatternly dresses, children with peaked faces, men unhappy and unshaven. A woman caught sight of my uniform. "Vive l'Angleterre," she cried, and they all came stumbling forward to embrace me. It was horrible. They creaked like automatons. They gestured and mouthed, but the soul had been crushed out of their eyes. You don't need any proofs of Hun atrocities; the proofs are to be seen at Evian. There are no severed hands, no crucified bodies; only hearts that have been mutilated. Sorrow is at its saddest when it cannot even contrive to appear dignified. There is no dignity about the repatries at Evian, with their absurd umbrellas, sauce-pans, patched-boots, alarm-clocks and bird-cages. They do not appeal to one as sacrificed patriots. There is no nobility in their vacant stare. They create a cold feeling of bodily decay - only it is the spirit that is dead and gangrenous.

There is a blasphemous story by Leonid Andreyev, which recounts the bitterness of the after years of Lazarus and the mischief Christ wrought in recalling him from the grave. After his unnatural return to life there was a blueness as of putrescence beneath his pallor; an iciness to his touch; a choking silence in his presence; a horror in his gaze, as if he were remembering his three days in the sepulchre - as if forbidden knowledge groped behind his eyes. He rarely looked at any one; there were none who courted his glance, who did not creep away to die. The terror of his fame spread beyond Bethany. Rome heard of him, and at that safe distance laughed. It did not laugh after Caesar Augustus had sent for him. Caesar Augustus was a god upon earth; he could not die. But when he had questioned Lazarus, peeped through the windows of his eyes, and read what lay hidden in that forbidden memory, he commanded that red-hot irons should quench such sight for ever. From Rome Lazarus groped his way back to Palestine and there, long years after his Saviour had been crucified, continued to stumble through his own particular Gethsemane of blindness. I thought of that story in the presence of this crowd, which carried with it the taint of the grave.

But the band was still playing the Marseillaise - over and over it played it. With each repetition it was as though these people, three years dead, made another effort to cast aside their shrouds. Little by little something was happening - something wonderful. Backs were straightening; skirts were being caught up; resolution was rippling from face to face - it passed and re-passed with each new roll of the drums. The hoarse cries and moaning with which we had commenced were gradually transforming themselves into singing.

There were some who were too weak to walk; these were carried by the American Red Cross men into the waiting ambulances. The remainder were marshalled into a disorderly procession and led out of the station by the band.

We were moving down the hill to the palaces beside the lake - the palaces to which all France used to troop for pleasure. We moved soddenly at first, shuffling in our steps. But the drums were still rolling out their defiance and the bugles were still blowing. The laziest man in the French Army was doing his utmost to belie his record. The ill-shod, flattened feet took up the music. They began to dance. Were there ever feet less suited to dancing? That they should dance was the acme of tragedy. Stockings fell down in creases about the ankles. Women commenced to jig their Boche babies in their arms; consumptive men and ancients waved their sauce-pans and grotesque bundles of umbrellas. The sight was damnable. It was a burlesque. It pierced the heart. What right had the Boche to leave these people so comic after he had squeezed the life-blood out of them?

All his insults to humanity became suddenly typified in these five hundred jumping tatterdemalions - the way in which he had plundered the world of its youth, its cleanness, its decency. I felt an anger which battlefields had never aroused, where men moulder above ground and become unsightly beneath the open sky. The slain of battlefields were at least motionless; they did not gape and grin at you with the dreadful humour of these perambulating dead. I felt the Galilean passion which animates every Red Cross worker at Evian: the agony to do something to make these murdered people live again. This last convoy came, I discovered, from a city behind the Boche lines against which last summer I had often directed fire. It was full in sight from my observing station. I had watched the very houses in which these people, who now walked beside me, had sheltered. For three and a half years these women's bodies had been at the Hun's mercy. I tried to bring the truth home to myself. Their men and young girls had been left behind. They themselves had been flung back on overburdened France only because they were no longer serviceable. They were returning actually penniless, though seemingly with money. The thrifty German makes a practice of seizing all the good redeemable French money of the repatries before he lets them escape him, giving them in exchange worthless paper stuff of his own manufacture, which has no security behind it and is therefore not negotiable.

We came to the Casino, where endless formalities were necessary. First of all in the big hall, formerly devoted to gambling, the repatries were fed at long tables. As I passed, odd groups seeing my uniform, hurriedly dropped whatever they were doing and, removing their caps, stood humbly at attention. There was fear in their promptness. Where they came from an officer exacted respect with the flat of his sword. What a dumb, helpless jumble of humanity! It was as though the occupants of a morgue had become galvanised and had temporarily risen from their slabs.

The band had been augmented by trumpets. It took its place in the gallery and deluged the hall with patriotic fervour. An old man climbed on a table and yelled, "Vive La France!" But they had grown tired of shouting; they soon grew tired. The cry was taken up faintly and soon exhausted itself. Nothing held their attention for long. Most of them sat hunched up and inert, weakly crying. They were not beautiful. They were not like our men who die in battle. They were animated memories of horror. "What lies before us? What lies before us?" That was the question that their silence asked perpetually. Some of them had husbands with the French army; others had sweethearts. What would those men say to the flaxen-haired babies who nestled against the women's breasts? And the sin was not theirs - they were such tired, pretty mites. "What lies before us?" The babies, too, might well have asked that question. Do you wonder that I at last began to share the

Frenchman's hatred for the Boche?

An extraordinary person in a white tie, top hat and evening dress entered. He looked like a cross between Mr. Gerard's description of himself in Berlin and a head-waiter. He evidently expected his advent to cause a profound sensation. I found out why: he was the official welcomer to Evian. Twice a day, for an infinity of days, he had entered in solemn fashion, faced the same tragic assembly, made the same fiery oration, gained applause at the climax of the same rounded periods and allowed his voice to break in the same rightly timed places. Having kept his audience in sufficient suspense as regards his mission, he unwrapped the muffler from his neck, removed his coat, felt his throat to see whether it was in good condition, swelled out his chest, including his waist-coat which was spanned by the broad ribbon of his office, then let loose the painter of his emotion and slipped off into the mid-stream of perfunctory eloquence. With all his disrobing he had retained his top-hat; he held it in his right hand with the brim pressed against his thigh, very much in the manner of a showman at a circus. It contributed largely to the opulence of his gestures.

He always seemed to have concluded and was always starting up afresh, as if in reluctant response to spectral clapping. He called upon the repatries never to forget the crimes that had been wrought against them - to spread abroad the fire of their indignation, the story of their ravished womanhood and broken families all over France. They watched him leaden-eyed and wept softly. To forget, to forget, that was all that they wanted - to blot out all the past. This man with the top-hat and the evening-dress, he hadn't suffered - how could he understand? They didn't want to remember; with those flaxen-haired children against their breasts the one boon they craved was forgetfulness. And so they cowered and wept softly. It was intolerable.

And now the formalities commenced. They all had to be medically examined. Questions of every description were asked them. They were drifted from bureau to bureau where people sat filling up official blanks. The Americans see to the children. They come from living in cellars, from conditions which are insanitary, from cities in the army zones where they were underfed. The fear is that they may spread contagion all over France. When infectious cases are found the remnants of families have to be broken up afresh. The mothers collapse on benches sobbing their hearts out as their children are led away. For three and a half years everything they have loved has been led away - how can they believe that these Americans mean only mercy?

From three to four hours are spent in completing all these necessary investigations. Before the repatries are conducted to their billets, all their clothes have to be disinfected and every one has to be bathed. The poor people are utterly worn out by the end of it - they have already done a continuous four days' journey in cramped trains. Before being sent to France they have been living for from two to three weeks in Belgium. The Hun always sends the repatries to Belgium for a few weeks before returning them. The reason for this is that they for the most part come from the army zones, and a few weeks will make any information they possess out of date. Another reason is that food is more plentiful in Belgium, thanks to the Allies' Relief Commission. These people have been kept alive on sugar-beets for the past few months, so it is as well to feed them at the Allies' expense for a little while, in order that they may create a better impression when they return to France. The American doctors pointed out to me the pulpy flesh of the children and the distended stomachs which, to the unpractised eye, seemed a sign of over-nourishment. "Wind and water," they said; "that's all these children are. They've no stamina. Sugar-beets are the most economic means of just keeping the body and the soul together."

The lights are going out in the Casino. It is the hour when, in the old days, life would be becoming most feverish about the gaming tables. In little forlorn groups the repatries are being conducted to their temporary quarters in the town. To-morrow morning before it is light, another train-load will arrive, the band will again play the Marseillaise, the American Red Cross workers will again be in attendance, the gentleman in the top-hat and white-tie will again make his fiery oration of welcome, his audience will again pay no attention but will weep softly - the tediously heart-rending scene will be rehearsed throughout in every detail by an entirely new batch of actors. Twice a day, summer and winter, the same tragedy is enacted at Evian. It is a continuous, never-ending performance.

Poor people! These whom I have seen, if they have no friends to claim them, will re-start their journey to some strange department on which they will be billeted as paupers. Here again the American Red Cross is doing good work, for it sends one of its representatives ahead to see that proper preparations have been made for their reception. After they have reached their destination, it looks them up from time to time to make sure that they are being well cared for.

If one wants to picture the case of the repatrie in its true misery, all he needs to do is to convert it into terms of his own mother or grandmother. She has lived all her life in the neighbourhood of Vimy, let us say. She was married there and it was there that she bore all her children. She and her husband have saved money; they are substantial people now and need not fear the future. Their sons are gaining their own living; one daughter is married, the others are arriving at the marriageable age. One day the Hun sweeps down on them. The sons escape to join the French army; the girls and their parents stay behind to guard their property. They are immediately evacuated from Vimy and sent to some city, such as Drocourt, further behind the Hun front-line. Here they are gradually robbed of all their possessions. At the beginning all their gold is confiscated; later even the mattresses upon their beds are requisitioned. For three and a half years they are subjected to both big and petty tyrannies, till their spirits are so broken that fear becomes their predominant emotion. The father is led away to work in the mines. One by one the daughters are commandeered and sent off into the heart of Germany, where it will be no one's business to guard their virtue. At last the mother is left with only her youngest child. Of her sons who are fighting with the French armies she has no knowledge, whether they are living or dead. Then one day it is decided by her captors that they have no further use for her. They part her from her last remaining child and pack her off by way of Belgium and Switzerland back to her own country. She arrives at Evian penniless and half-witted with the terror of her sorrow. There is no one to claim her; the part of France that knew her is all behind the German lines. A label is tied to her, as if she was a piece of baggage, and she is shipped off to Avignon, let us say. She has never been in the South before; it is a foreign country to her. Poverty and adversity have broken her pride; she has nothing left that will command respect. There is nothing left in life to which she can fasten her affections. Such utter forlornness is never a welcome sight. Is it to be wondered at that the strangers to whom she is sent are not always glad to see her? Is it to be wondered at that, after her repatriation, she often wilts and dies? Her sorrow has the appearance of degradation. Wherever she goes, she is a threat and a peril to the fighting morale of the civilian population. Yet in her pre-war kindliness and security she might have been your mother or mine.

The American Red Cross, by maintaining contact with such people, is keeping them reminded that they are not utterly deserted - that the whole of civilised humanity cares tremendously what becomes of them and is anxious to lighten the load of their sacrifice.

*　*　*　*　*

I have before me a pile of sworn depositions, made by exiles returned from the invaded territories. They are separately numbered and dated; each bears the name of the region or town from which the repatrie came. Here are a few extracts which, when pieced together, form a picture of the life of captured French civilians behind the German lines. I have carefully avoided glaring atrocities. Atrocities are as a rule isolated instances, due to isolated causes. They occur, but they are not typical of the situation. The real Hun atrocity is the attitude towards life which calls chivalry sentiment, fair-play a waste of opportunity and ruthlessness strength. This attitude is all summed up in the one word Prussianism. The repatries have been Prussianised out of their wholesome joy and belief in life; it is this that makes them the walking accusations that they are to-day. In the following depositions they give some glimpses of the calculated processes by which their happiness has been murdered.

*　*　*　*　*

"Lately copper, tin, and zinc have been removed in the factories and amongst the traders, and quite recently in private houses. For all these requisitions the Germans gave Requisition Bonds, but private individuals who received them never got paid the money. To force men to work 'voluntarily' and sign contracts the Germans employed the following means: the Germans gave these men nothing to eat, but authorised their families to send them parcels; these parcels once in the hands of the Germans are shown to these unhappy men and are not handed over until they have signed. About a week ago young boys from the age of fourteen who had come back from the Ardennes had to present themselves at the Kdr to be registered anew; a number of the young people work in the sawmills, etc.; some have died of privation and fatigue."

*　*　*　*　*

"A week after Easter this year the population of LILLE was warned by poster that all must be ready to leave the town. At three o'clock in the morning private houses were invaded by the German soldiers; they sorted out women and girls who were to be deported. There then took place scandalous scenes: young girls belonging to the most worthy families in the town had to pass medical visits even with the speculum and had to endure most atrocious physical and moral suffering. These young girls were segregated like beasts anywhere in the rooms of the town halls and schoolhouses, and were mingled with the dregs of the population."

*   *   *   *   *

"For a certain time the Germans did not requisition milk and allowed it to be sold, but now this is forbidden under a fine of 1,000 marks or three months' imprisonment. Recently WIGNEHIES was fined 100,000 frcs., and as the whole of this sum was not paid the Germans inflicted punishment as follows: Several inhabitants of WIGNEHIES were caught in the act of disobeying by the gendarmes and were struck, and bitten by the police dogs of the gendarmes because they refused to denounce the sellers.... Brutal treatment is due more to the gendarmes than to the soldiers. About six weeks ago Marceau Horlet of WIGNEHIES was found, on a search by the gendarmes, to have a piece of meat in his possession. He was brutally beaten by them and bitten by the police dogs because he refused to say who had given it to him. In 1915, the youth Remy Vallei of WIGNEHIES, age 15, was walking in the street after 6-9 p.m., which was forbidden; he was seen by two gendarmes and ran away. He was straightway killed, receiving six revolver bullets in his body."

*   *   *   *   *

"At PIGNICOURT during the CHAMPAGNE offensive the village was bombarded by the French, who were attempting to destroy the railway lines and bridges. The Commandant, by name Krama, of the Kdr, forced men and youths, and even women, to fill up the holes made by the bombardment during the action. A German general passed and reprimanded them on the ground that there was danger to the civilians; they were withdrawn for the moment, but sent back as soon as the general had left."

*   *   *   *   *

"As regards the Hispano-American revictualling, it may be said with truth that without this the population of Northern France would have died of hunger, for the Germans considered themselves liberated from any responsibility. During the first months of the war before this Committee started, the Germans put up posters saying that the Allies were trying to starve Germany, who in turn was not obliged to feed the invaded territory.... When informant (who is from ST. QUENTIN) left at the general evacuation of this town, no requisition bonds were given for household goods. As the inhabitants left, their furniture was loaded on to motor lorries and taken to the station, whence it was sent by special train to Germany. This shows clearly that requisition bonds issued by the Germans show only the small proportion of what has been suffered by the inhabitants.... Informant was the witness of the execution of French civilians whose only fault was either to hide arms or pigeons: several who had committed these infractions of requisitions were shot, and the Germans announced the fact by poster of a blood-red colour. In other cases the men shot were British prisoners who had dressed in civil clothes on the arrival of the Germans. Informant had a long conversation with one of them before his execution. He told informant how he had been unable to leave ST. QUENTIN, viz., by the 28th August. Some passers-by offered to hide him. It appears that, through his ignorance of the French language, he was unaware that the Germans threatened execution to all men found after a certain date. He was discovered and condemned to death for espionage. It is obvious, as the man himself said, that one could not imagine a man acting as a spy without knowing either the language of the country or that of the enemy."

*　*　*　*　*

"Before the evacuation of the population the Germans chose those who were to remain as civilian workers, viz., 120 men from 15 to 60. On the very day of the evacuation they kept back at the station 27 others. These men are now at CANTIN or SOMAIN, where they are employed on the roads or looking after munitions in the Arras group. The others at DECHY and GUESNIN are in the VIMY group and are making pill-boxes or railway lines. A certain number of these workers refused to carry out the work ordered, and as punishment during the summer were tied to chairs and exposed bareheaded to the full blaze of the sun. They were often threatened to be shot."

*   *   *   *   *

"After the bombardment of LILLE the Germans entered ENNETIERES on the 12th October, 1914. On the next Monday 200 Uhlans occupied the Commune, and houses and haystacks were burned.... At LOMME every one was forced to work: the Saxon Kdnt. Schoper announced that all women who did not obey within 24 hours would be interned: all the women obeyed. They were employed in the making of osier-revetement two metres high for the trenches. The men were forced to put up barbed wire near Fort Denglas, two kltrs. from the front. A few days after the evacuation of ENNET-IERES the Uhlans shot a youth, Jean Leclercq, age 17, son of the gardener of Count D'Hespel, simply because they had found a telephone wire in the courtyard of the chateau."

*   *   *   *   *

"Informant, who has lost his right arm, was nevertheless forced to work for the Germans, notably to unload coal and to work on the roads. He had with him males from 13 to 60. Having objected because of his lost arm, he was threatened with imprisonment. At LOMME squads of workers were given the work of putting up barbed wire; women were forced to make sand bags. In cases of refusal on either side the Kdr. inflicted four or five weeks' imprisonment, to say nothing of blows with sticks inflicted by the soldiers. In spring 1917 a number of men were sent from LOMME to the BEAUVIN-PROVINS region to work on defences.... Those who refused to sign were threatened and struck with the butts of rifles, and left in cellars sometimes filled with water during bombardments. Several of them came back seriously ill from privation."

*   *   *   *   *

"Young girls are separated from their mothers; there are levies made at every moment. Sometimes these young girls have barely a few hours before the moment of departure.... Several young girls have written to say that they are very unhappy and that they sleep in camps amongst girls of low class and condition."

*   *   *   *   *

"For a long time past women have been forced to work as road labourers. These work in the quarries and transport wood cut down by the men in the mountain forest. A number of women and young girls have been removed from their families and sent in the direction of RHEIMS and RETHEL, where it is said (although this cannot be confirmed) that they are employed in aerodromes."

*   *   *   *   *

These extracts should serve to explain the mental and physical depression of the returning exiles. They have been bullied out of the desire to live and out of all possession of either their bodies or their souls. They have been treated like cattle, and as cattle they have come to regard themselves. Lazaruses - that's what they are! The unmerciful Boche, having killed and buried them, drags them out from the tomb and compels them to go through the antics of life. Le Gallienne's poem comes to my mind:

> "Loud mockers in the angry street
> Say Christ is crucified again -
> Twice pierced those gospel-bearing feet,
> Twice broken that great heart in vain...."

That is all true at Evian. But when I see the American men and girls, leaning over the Boche babies in their cots and living their hearts into the hands and feet of the spiritually maimed, the last two lines of the poem become true for me:

Coningsby Dawson

"I hear, and to myself I say,
'Why, Christ walks with me every day.'"

The work of the American Red Cross at Evian is largely devoted to children. It provides all the ambulance transportation for the repatries, to and from the station. American doctors and nurses do all the examining of the children at the Casino. On an average, four hundred pass through their hands daily. The throat, nose, teeth, glands and skin of each child are inspected. If the child is suspected or attacked by any disease, it is immediately segregated and sent to the American hospital. If the infection is only local or necessitates further examination, the child and its family are summoned to present themselves at the American dispensary next day. Every precaution is employed to prevent the spread of infection - particularly the infection of tuberculosis. Evian is the gateway from Germany through which disease and death may be carried to the furthest limits of France. Very few of the repatries are really healthy. It would be a wonder if they were after the privations through which they have passed. All of them are weakened in vitality and broken down in stamina. Many of them have no homes to go to and have to be sent to departments of the interior and the south. If they were sent in an unhealthy condition, it would mean the spread of epidemics.

The Red Cross has a large children's hospital at Evian in the villas and buildings of the Hotel Chatelet. This hospital deals with the contagious cases. It has others, especially one at the Chateau des Halles, thirty kilometers from Lyons, which take the devitalised, convalescent and tubercular cases. The Chateau des Halles is a splendidly built modern building, arranged in an ideal way for hospital use. It stands at the head of a valley, with an all day sun exposure and large grounds. Close to the Chateau are a number of small villages in which it is possible to lodge the repatries in families. This is an important part of the repatrie's problem, as after their many partings they fight fiercely against any further separations. One of the chief reasons for having the Convalescent Hospital out in the country is that families can be quartered in the villages and so kept together.

The pathetic hunger of these people for one another after they have been so long divided, was illustrated for me on my return journey to Paris. A man of the tradesman class had been to Evian to meet his wife and his boy of about eleven. They were among the lucky ones, for they had a home to go to. He was not prepossessing in appearance. He had a weak face, lined with anxiety, broken teeth and limp hair. His wife, as so often happens in French marriages, had evidently been the manageress. She was unbeautiful in rusty black; her clothes were the ill-assorted make-shifts of the civilian who escapes from Germany. Her eyes were shifty with the habit of fear and sunken with the weariness of crying. The boy was a bright little fellow, full of defiance and anecdotes of his recent captors.

When I entered the carriage, they were sitting huddled together - the man in the middle, with an arm about either of them. He kept pressing them to him, kissing them by turn in a spasmodic unrestrained fashion, as if he still feared that he might lose them and could not convince himself of the happy truth that they were once again together. The woman did not respond to his embraces; she seemed indifferent to him, indifferent to life, indifferent to any prospects. The boy seemed fond of his father, but embarrassed by his starved demonstrativeness.

I listened to their conversation. The man's talk was all of the future - what splendid things he would do for them. How, as long as they lived, he would never waste a moment from their sides. It appeared that he had been at Tours, on a business trip when the war broke out, and could not get back to Lille before the Germans arrived there. For three and a half years he had lived in suspense, while everything he loved had lain behind the German lines. The woman contributed no suggestions to his brilliant plans. She clung to him, but she tried to divert his affection. When she spoke it was of small domestic abuses: the exorbitant prices she had had to pay for food; the way in which the soldiery had stolen her pots and pans; the insolence she had experienced when she had lodged complaints against the men before their officers. And the boy - he wanted to be a poilu. He kept inventing revenges he would take in battle, if the war lasted long enough for his class to be called out. As darkness fell they ceased talking. I began to realise that in three and a half years they had lost contact. They were saying over and over the things that had been said already; they were trying to prevent themselves from acknowledging that they had grown different and separate. The only bond which held them as a family was their common loneliness and fear that, if they did not hold together, their intolerable loneliness would return. When the light was hooded, the boy sank his hand against his father's shoulder; the woman nestled herself in the fold of his arm, with her head turned away from him, that he might not kiss her so often. The man sat upright, his eyes wide open, watching them sleeping with a kind of impotent despair. They were together; and yet they were not together. He had recovered them; nevertheless, he had not recovered them. Those Boches, the devils, they had kept something; they had only sent their bodies back. All night long, whenever I woke up as the train halted, the little man was still guarding them jealously as a dog guards a bone, and staring morosely at the blank wall of the future.

These were among the lucky ones; the boy and woman had had a man to meet them. Somewhere in France there was protection awaiting them and the shelter of a house that was not charity. And yet ... all night while they slept the man sat awake, facing up to facts. These were among the lucky ones! That is Evian; that is the tragedy and need of France as you see it embodied in individuals.

*   *   *   *   *

The total number of repatries and refugies now in France is said to total a million and a half. The repatries are the French civilians who were captured by the Germans in their advance and have since been sent back. The refugies are the French civilians from the devastated areas, who have always remained on the Allies' side of the line. The refugies are divided into two classes: refugies proper - that is fugitives from the front, who fled for the most part at the time of the German invasion; and evacues - those who were sent out of the war zone by the military authorities. Naturally a large percentage of this million and a half have lost everything and, irrespective of their former worldly position, now live with the narrowest margin between themselves and starvation. The French Government has treated them with generosity, but in the midst of a war it has had little time to devote to educating them into being self-supporting. A great number of funds have been privately raised for them in France; many separate organisations for their relief have been started. The American Red Cross is making this million and a half people its special care, and to do so is co-operating directly with the French Government and with existing French civilian projects. Its action is dictated by mercy and admiration, but in results this policy is the most far-seeing statesmanship. A million and a half plundered people, if neglected and allowed to remain downhearted, are likely to constitute a danger to the morale of the bravest nation. Again, from the point of view of after-war relations, to have been generous towards those who have suffered is to have won the heart of France. The caring for the French repatriates and refugees is a definite contribution to the winning of the war.

The French system of handling this human stream of tragedy is to send the sick to local hospitals and the exhausted to the *maison de repos*. The comparatively healthy are allowed to be claimed by friends; the utterly homeless are sent to some prefecture remote from the front-line. The prefects in turn distribute them among towns and villages, lodging them in old barracks, casinos and any buildings which war-conditions have made vacant. The adults are allowed by the Government a franc and a half per day, and the children seventy-five centimes.

The armies have drained France of her doctors since the war; until the Americans came, the available medical attention was wholly inadequate to the civilian population. The American

Red Cross is now establishing dispensaries through the length and breadth of France. In country districts, inaccessible to towns, it is inaugurating automobile-dispensaries which make their rounds on fixed and advertised days. In addition to this it has started a child-welfare movement, the aim of which is to build up the birth-rate and lower the infant mortality by spreading the right kind of knowledge among the women and girls.

The condition of the refugees and repatriates, thrust into communities to which they came as paupers and crowded into buildings which were never planned for domestic purposes, has been far from enviable. In September, 1917, the American Red Cross handed over the solving of this problem to one of its experts who had organised the aid given to San Francisco after the earthquake, and who had also had charge of the relief-work necessitated by the Ohio floods at Dayton. Co-operating with the French, houses partially constructed at the outbreak of war were now completed and furnished, and approximately three thousand families were supplied with homes and privacy. The start made proved satisfactory. Supplies, running into millions of francs, were requisitioned, and the plan for getting the people out of public buildings into homes was introduced to the officials of most of the departments of France. Delegates were sent out by the Red Cross to undertake the organisation of the work. Money was apportioned for the supplying of destitute families with furniture and the instruments of trade; the object in view was not to pauperise them, but to afford them the opportunity for becoming self-supporting. Reconstruction work in those devastated areas which have been won back from the Boche was hurried forward in order that the people who had been uprooted from the soil might be returned to it and, in being returned to their own particular soil, might recover their place in life and their balance.

I visited the devastated areas of the Pas-de-Calais, Somme, Oise and Aisne and saw what is being accomplished. This destroyed territory is roughly one hundred miles long by thirty miles broad at its widest point. In 1912 one-quarter of the wheat produced in France and eighty-seven per cent. of the beet crop employed in the national industry of sugar-making, were raised in these departments of the north. The invasion has diminished the national wheat production by more than a half. It is obvious, then, that in getting these districts once more under cultivation two birds are being killed with one stone: the refugee is being made a self-supporting person - an economic asset instead of a dead weight - and the tonnage problem is being solved. If more food is grown behind the Western Front, grain-ships can be released for transporting the munitions of war from America.

The French Government had already made a start in this undertaking before America came into the war. As early as 1914 it voted three hundred million francs and appointed a group of *sous-préfets* to see to the dispensing of it. Little by little, as the Huns have been driven back, the wealthier inhabitants, whose money was safe in Paris banks, have returned to these districts and opened *oeuvres* for the poorer inhabitants. Many of them have lost their sons and husbands; they find in their daily labour for others worse off than themselves an escape from life-long despair. Misfortune is a matter of comparison and contrast. We are all of us unhappy or fortunate according to our standards of selfishness and our personal interpretation of our lot. These patriots are bravely turning their experience of sorrow into the materials of service. They can speak the one and only word which makes a bond of sympathy between the prosperous and the broken-hearted, "I, too, have suffered." I came across one such woman in the neighbourhood of Villequier-au-Mont. She was a woman of title and a royalist. Her estates had been laid waste by the invasion and all her men-folk, save her youngest son, were dead. Directly the Hun withdrew last spring, she came back to the wilderness which had been created and commenced to spend what remained of her fortune upon helping her peasants. These peasants had been the hewers of wood and drawers of water for the Hun for three and a half years. When his armies retreated, they took with them the girls and the young men, leaving behind only the weaklings, the children and the aged. Word came to the Red Cross official of the district that her remaining son had been killed in action; he was asked to break the news to her. He went out to her ruined village and found her sitting among a group of women in the shell of a house, teaching them to make garments for their families. She was pleased to see him; she was in need of more materials. She had been intending to make the journey to see him herself. She was full of her work and enthusiastic over the valiance of her people. He led her aside and told her. She fell silent. Her face quivered - that was all. Then she completed her list of requirements and went back to her women. In living to comfort other people's grief, she had no time to nurse her own.

These "oeuvres," or groups of workers, settle down in a shattered village or township. The military authorities place the township in their charge. They at once commence to get roofs on to such houses as still have walls. They supply farm-implements, poultry, rabbits, carts, seeds, plants, etc. They import materials from Paris and form sewing classes for the women and girls. They encourage the trades-people to re-start their shops and lend them the necessary initial capital. What is perhaps most valuable, they lure the terror-stricken population out of their caves and dug-outs, and set them an example of hope and courage. Some of the best pioneer work of this sort has been done by the English Society of Friends who now, together with the Friends of the United States, have become a part of the Bureau of the Department of Civil Affairs of the American Red Cross.

The American Red Cross works through the "oeuvres" which it found already operating in the devastated area; it places its financial backing at their disposal, its means of motor transport and its personnel; it grafts on other "oeuvres," operating in newly taken over villages, in which Americans, French and English work side by side for the common welfare; at strategic points behind the lines it has established a chain of relief warehouses, fully equipped with motor-lorries and cars. These warehouses furnish everything that an agricultural people starting life afresh can require - food, clothes, blankets, beds, mattresses, stoves, kitchen utensils, reapers, binders, mowing-machines, threshing-machines, garden-tools, soap, tooth brushes, etc. If you can conceive of yourself as having been a prosperous farmer and waking up one morning broken in heart and dirty in person, with your barns, live-stock, daughters, sons, everything gone - not a penny left in the world - you can imagine your necessities, and then form some picture of the fore-thought that goes to the running of a Red Cross warehouse.

But the poverty of these people is not the worst condition that the Red Cross workers have to tackle; money can always replace money. Hope, trust, affection and a genial belief in the world's goodness cannot be transplanted into another man's heart in exchange for bitterness by even the most lavish giver. I can think of no modern parallel for their blank despair; the only eloquence which approximately expresses it is that of Job, centuries old, "Why is light given to a man whose way is hid and whom God hath hedged in? My sighing cometh before I eat. My roarings are poured out like waters. My harp is turned to mourning, and my organ into the voice of them that weep. I was not in safety, neither had I rest, neither was I quiet; yet trouble came."

This hell which the Hun has created, beggars any description of Dante.[1] It is still more appalling to remember that the external hell which one sees, does not represent one tithe of the dreariness which lies hidden behind the eyes of the inhabitants. To imagine amid such scenes is to paralyse compassion with agony. The craving, never far from one's thoughts, is the age-old desire, "O that one might plead with God, as a man pleadeth for his neighbour!"

[Footnote 1: Since this was written and just as I am returning to the front, the Hun has set to work to create this hell for the second time. Most of the places referred to below are once more within the enemy country and all the mercy of the American Red Cross has been wiped out.]

Coningsby Dawson

I started out on my trip in a staff-car from a city well behind the lines. In the first half hour of the journey the country was green and pleasant. We passed some cavalry officers galloping across a brown field; birds were battling against a flurrying wind; high overhead an aeroplane sailed serenely. There was a sense of life, motion and exhilaration abroad, but only for the first half hour of our journey. Then momentarily a depression grew up about us. Fields and trees were becoming dead, as if a swarm of locusts had eaten their way across them. Greenness was vanishing. Houses were becoming untenanted; there were holes in the walls of many of them, through which one gained glimpses of the sky. Here, by the road-side, we passed a cluster of insignificant graves. Then, almost without warning, the barbed-wire entanglements commenced, and the miles and miles of abandoned trenches. This, not a year ago from the day on which I write, was the Hun's country. Last spring, in an attempt to straighten his line, he retreated from it. Our offensives on the Somme had converted his Front into a dangerous salient.

We are slowing down; the road is getting water-logged and full of holes. The skull of a dead town grows up on the horizon. Even at this distance the light behind empty windows glares malevolently like the nothingness in vacant sockets. A horror is over everything. The horror is not so much due to the destruction as to the total absence of any signs of life. One man creeping through the landscape would make it seem more kindly. I have been in desolated towns often, but there were always the faces of our cheery Tommies to smile out from cellars and gaps in the walls. From here life is banished utterly. The battle-line has retired eastward; one can hear the faint rumble of the guns at times. No civilian has come to re-inhabit this unhallowed spot.

We enter what were once its streets. They are nothing now but craters with boards across them. On either side the trees lie flat along the ground, sawn through within a foot of the roots. What landmarks remain are the blackened walls of houses, cracked and crashed in by falling roofs. The entire place must have been given over to explosion and incendiarism before the Huns departed. One stands in awe of such completeness of savagery; one begins to understand what is meant by the term "frightfulness." As far as eye can reach there is nothing to be seen but decayed fangs, protruding from a swamp of filth, covered with a green slime where water has accumulated. This is not the unavoidable ruin of shell-fire. No battle was fought here. The demolition was the wanton spite of an enemy who, because he could not hold the place, was determined to leave nothing serviceable behind. With such masterly thoroughness has he done his work that the spot can never be re-peopled. The surrounding fields are too poisoned and churned up for cultivation. The French Government plans to plant a forest; it is all that can be done. As years go by, the kindliness of Nature may cause her to forget and cover up the scars of hatred with greenness. Then, perhaps, peasant lovers will wander here and refashion their dreams of a chivalrous world. Our generation will be dead by that time; throughout our lives this memorial to "frightfulness" will remain.

We have left the town and are out in the open country. It is clean and unharried. Man can murder orchards and habitations - the things which man plants and makes; he finds it more difficult to strangle the primal gifts of Nature. All along by the roadside the cement telegraph-posts have been broken off short; some of them lie flat along the ground, others hang limply in the bent shape of hairpins. Very often we have to make a detour where a steel bridge has been blown up; we cross the gulley over an improvised affair of struts and planks, and so come back into the main roadway. Every now and then we pass steam-tractors at work, ploughing huge fields into regular furrows. The French Department of Agriculture purchased in America nineteen teams of ten tractors apiece in the autumn of last year. The American Red Cross has supplied others. The fields of this district are unfenced - the farmers used to live together in villages; so the work is made easy. It is possible to throw a number of holdings together and to apply to France the same wholesale mechanical means of wheat-growing that are employed on the prairies of Canada. All the cattle and horses have been carried off into Germany. All the farm-implements have been destroyed - and destroyed with a surprising ingenuity. The same parts were destroyed in each instrument, so that an entire instrument could not be reconstructed. The farms could nothave been brought under cultivation this year, had not the Government and the Red Cross lent their assistance.

We are approaching Noyon, the birthplace of Calvin. This is one of the few towns the Hun spared in his retreat; he spared it not out of a belated altruism, but purely to serve his own convenience. There were some of the French civilians who weren't worth transporting to Germany. They would be too weak, or too old, or too young to earn their keep when he got them there. These he sorted out, irrespective of their family ties, and herded from the surrounding districts into Noyon. They were crowded into the houses and ordered under pain of death not to come out until they were given permission. They were further ordered to shutter all their windows and not to look out.

As an old lady, who narrated the story, said, "We had no idea, Monsieur, what was to happen. *Les Boches* had been with us for nearly three years; it never entered our heads that they were leaving. When they took the last of our young girls from us and all who were strong among our men, it was something that they had done so often and so often. When they made us hide in our houses, we thought it was only to prevent a disturbance. It is not easy to see your boys and girls marched away into slavery - Monsieur will understand that. Sometimes, on former occasions, the mothers had attacked *les Boches* and the young girls had become hysterical; we thought that it was to avoid such scenes that we were shut up in our houses. When darkness fell, we sat in our rooms without any lights, for they also were forbidden. All night long through our streets we heard the endless tramping of battalions, the clattering wheels of guns and limbers, the sharp orders, the halting and the marching taken up afresh. Toward s dawneverything grew silent. At first it would be broken occasionally by the hurried trot of cavalry or the shuffling footsteps of a straggler. Then it grew into the absolute silence of death. It was nerve-racking and terrible. One could almost hear the breathing of the listening people in all the other houses. I do not know how time went or what was the hour. I could endure the suspense no longer. They might kill me, but ... Ah well, at my age after nearly three years with 'les Boches,' killing is a little matter! I crept down the passage and drew back the bolts. I was very gentle; a sentry might hear me. I opened the door just a crack. I expected to hear a rifle-shot ring out, but nothing happened. I opened it wider, and saw that the street was empty and that it was broad daylight. Then I waited - I do not know how long I waited. I crouched against the wall, huddled with terror. All this took much longer in the doing than in the telling. At last I could bear myself no longer. I tiptoed out on to the pavement - and, Monsieur will believe me, I expected to drop dead. But no one disturbed me. Then I heard a rustling. Doors everywhere were opening stealthily, ah, so stealthily! Some one else tiptoed out, and some one else, and some one else. We stood there staring, aghast at our daring. Suddenly we realised what had happened. The brutes had gone. We were free. It was indescribable, what followed - we ran together, weeping and embracing. At first we wept for gladness; soon we wept for sorrow. Our youth had departed; we were all old women or very ancient men. Two hours later our poilus came, like a blue-grey wave of laughter, fighting their way through the burning country that those swine had left in a sea of smoke and flames."

And so that was why the Hun spared Noyon. But if he spared Noyon, he spared little else.[2] Every village between here and the present front line has been levelled; every fruit-tree cut down. The wilful wickedness and pettiness of the crime stir one's heart to pity and his soul to white-hot anger. The people who did this must make payment in more than money; to settle such a debt blood is required. American soldiers who came to Europe to do a job and with no decided detestation of the Hun, are being taught by such landscapes. They know now why they came. The wounds of France are educating them.

Coningsby Dawson

[Footnote 2: Goodness knows where the "present Front-line" may be by the time this book is published. I visited Noyon in February, 1918, just before the big Hun offensive commenced.]

There has been a scheme proposed in America under which certain individual cities and towns in the States shall make themselves responsible for the re-building of certain individual cities and towns in the devastated areas. The scheme is noble; it has only one drawback, namely that it specialises effort and tends to ignore the immensity of the problem as a whole. I visited one of these towns - it is a town for which Philadelphia has made itself responsible. I wish the people of Philadelphia might get a glimpse of the task they have undertaken. There is a church-spire still standing; that is about all. The rest is a pile of bricks. In the midst of this havoc some Philadelphia ladies are living, one of whom is a nurse. They run a dispensary for the people who keep house for the most part in cellars and holes in the ground. A doctor visits them to hold a clinic ever so often. They have a little warehouse, in which they keep the necessities for immediate relief work. They have a rest hut for soldiers. They employ whatever civilian labour they can hire for the roofing of some of the least damaged cottages; for this temporary reconstruction they provide the materials. When I was there, the place was well within range of enemy shell-fire. The approach had to be made by way of camouflaged roads. The sole anxiety of these brave women was that on account of their nearness to the front-line, the military might compel them to move back. In order to safeguard themselves against this and to create a good impression, they were making a strong point of entertaining whatever officers were billeted in this vicinity. Their effort to remain in this rural Gomorrah was as courageous as it was pathetic. "The people need us," they said, and then, "you don't think we'll be moved back, do you?" I thought they would, and I didn't think that the grateful officers would be able to prevent it - they were subalterns and captains for the most part. "But we once had a major to tea," they said. "A major!" I exclaimed, trying to look impressed, "Oh well, that makes a difference!"

There was one unit I wished especially to visit; it was a unit consisting entirely of women, sent over and financed by a women's college. When I was in America last October and heard that they were starting, I made up my mind that they were doomed to disappointment. I pictured the battlefield of the Somme as I had last seen it - a sea of mud stretching for miles, furrowed by the troughs of battered trenches, pitted every yard with shell-holes and smeared over with the wreckage of what once were human bodies. I could not imagine what useful purpose women could serve amid such surroundings. It seemed to me indecent that they should be allowed to go there. They were going to do reconstruction, I was told. Reconstruction! you can't reconstruct towns and villages the very foundations of which have been buried. There is a Bible phrase which expresses such annihilation, "The place thereof shall know it no more." Yes, only the names remain in one's memory - the very sites have been covered up and the contours of the landscape re-dug with high explosives. It took millions of pounds to work this havoc. Men tunnelled under-ground and sprung mines without warning. They climbed like birds of prey, into the heavens to hurl death from the clouds. They lined up their guns, tier upon tier, almost axle to axle in places, and at a given sign rained a deluge of corruption on a country miles in front, which they could not even discern. The infantry went over the top throwing bombs and piled themselves up into mounds of silence. Nations far away toiled day and night in factories - and all that they might achieve this repellant desolation. The innocence of the project made one smile - a handful of women sailing from America to reconstruct! To reconstruct will take ten times more effort than was required to destroy. More than eight hundred years ago William the Norman burnt his way through the North Country to Chester. Yorkshire has not yet recovered; it is still a wind-swept moorland. This women's college in America hoped to repair in our lifetime a ruin a million times more terrible. Their courage was depressing, it so exceeded the possible. They might love one village back to life, but.... That is exactly what they are doing.

Coningsby Dawson

I arrived at Grecourt on an afternoon in January. It is here that he women of the Smith College Unit have taken up their tenancy. We had extraordinary difficulty in finding the place. The surrounding country had been blasted and scorched by fire. There was no one left of whom we could enquire. Everything had perished. Barns, houses, everything habitable had been blown up by the departing Hun. As a study in the painstaking completion of a purpose the scenes through which we passed almost called for admiration. Berlin had ordered her armies to destroy everything before withdrawing; they had obeyed with a loving thoroughness. The world has never seen such past masters in the art of demolition. Ever since they invaded Belgium, their hand has been improving. In the neighbourhood of Grecourt they have equalled, if not surpassed, their own best efforts. I would suggest to the Kaiser that this manly performance calls for a distribution of iron crosses. It is true that his armies were beaten and retiring; but does not that fact rather enhance their valour? They were retiring, yet there were those who were brave enough to delay their departure till they had achieved this final victory over old women and children to the lasting honour of their country. Such heroes are worthy to stand beside the sinkers of the *Lusitania*. It is not just that they should go unrecorded.

In the midst of this hell I came across a tumbled chateau. Its roof, its windows, its stairways were gone; only the crumbling shell of its former happiness was left standing. A high wall ran about its grounds. The place must have been pleasant with flower-gardens once. There was an impressive entrance of wrought-iron, a porter's lodge and a broad driveway. At the back I found rows of little wood-huts. There was a fragrance of log-fires burning. I was glad of that, for I had heard of the starving cold these women had had to endure through the first winter months of their tenure. On tapping at a door, I found the entire colony assembled. It was tea-time and Sunday. Ten out of the seventeen who form the colony were present. A box-stove, such as we use in our pioneer shacks in Canada, was throwing out a glow of cheeriness. Candles had been lighted. Little knicknacks of feminine taste had been hung here and there to disguise the bareness of the walls. A bed, in one corner, was carefully disguised as a couch. Save for the fact that there was no glass in the window - glass being unobtainable in France at present - one might easily have persuaded himself that he was back in America in the room of a girl-undergraduate.

The method of my greeting furthered this illusion. Americans, both men and women, have an extraordinary self-poise, a gift for remaining normal in the most abnormal surroundings. They refuse to allow themselves to be surprised by any upheaval of circumstances. "I should worry," they seem to be saying, and press straight on with the job in hand. There was one small touch which made the environment seem even more friendly and unexceptional. One of the girls, on being introduced, promptly read to me a letter which she had just received from my sister in America. It made this oasis in an encircling wilderness seem very much a part of a neighbourly world. This girl is an example of the varied experiences which have trained American women into becoming the nursemaids of the French peasantry.

She was visiting relations in Liege when the war broke out. On the Sunday she went for a walk on the embattlements and was turned back. Baulked in this direction, she strolled out towards the country and found men digging trenches. That was the first she knew that war was rumoured. On the Tuesday, two days later, Hun shells were detonating on the house-tops. She was held prisoner in Liege for some months after the Forts had fallen and saw more than all the crimes against humanity that the Bryce Report has recorded. At last she disguised herself and contrived her escape into Holland. From there she worked her way back to America and now she is at Grecourt, starting shops in the villages, educating the children, and behaving generally as if to respond to the "Follow thou me" of the New Testament was an entirely unheroic proceeding for a woman.

And what are these women doing at Grecourt? To condense their purpose into a phrase, I should say that by their example they are bringing sanity back into the lives of the French peasants. That is what the American Fund for French Wounded is doing at Blerancourt, what all these reconstruction units are doing in the devastated areas, and what the American Red Cross is doing on a much larger scale for the whole of France. At Grecourt they have a dispensary and render medical aid. If the cases are grave, they are sent to the American Hospital at Nesle. They hunt out the former tradespeople among the refugees and encourage them to re-start their shops, lending them the money for the purpose. If the men are captives in Germany, then their wives are helped to carry on the business in their absence and for their sakes. Groups of mothers are brought together and set to work on making clothes for themselves and their children. Schools are opened so that the children may be more carefully supervised. Two of the girls at Grecourt have learnt to plough, and are instructing the peasant women. Cows are kept and a dairy has been started to provide the under-nourished babies of the district. An automobile-dispensary is sent out from the hospital at Nesle to visit the remoter districts. It has a seat along one side for the patient and the nurse. Over the seat is a rack for medicine and instruments. On the opposite side is a rack for splints and surgical dressings. On the floor of the car a shower-bath is arranged, which is so compact that it can be carried into the house where the water is to be heated. The water is put into a tub on a wooden base; while the doctor manipulates the pump for the shower, the nurse does the scrubbing. Most of the diseases among the children are due to dirt; the importance of keeping clean, which such colonies as that at Grecourt are impressing on all the people whom they serve, is doing much to improve the general state of health. In this direction, as in so many others, the most valuable contribution that they are making to their districts is not material and financial, but mental - the contribution of example and suggestion. Seventeen women cannot re-build in a day an external civilisation which has been blotted out by the savagery of a nation; but they can and they are re-building the souls of the human derelicts who have survived the savagery. This war is going to be won not by the combination of nations which has most men and guns, but by the side which possesses the highest spiritual qualities. The same is true of the countries which will wipe out the effects of war most quickly when the war is ended. The first countries to recover will be those which fight on in a new way, after peace has been signed, for the same ideals for which they have shed their blood. The sight of these American women, living helpfully and voluntarily for the sake of others among hideous surroundings, is a perpetual reminder to the dispirited refugees that, whatever else is lost, valiance and loyalty still survive.

From Grecourt I went farther afield to Croix, Y and Matigny. Here a young architect is in charge of the reconstruction. No attempt is being made at present to re-build the farms entirely. Labour is difficult to obtain - it is all required for military purposes. The same applies to materials. Patching is the best that can be done. Just to get a roof over one corner of a ruin is as much as can be hoped for. Until that is done the people have to live in cellars, in shell-holes, in verminous dug-outs like beasts of prey or savages. Their position is far more deplorable than that of Indians, for they once knew the comforts of civilisation. For instance, I visited a farmer who before the war was a millionaire in French money. Many of the farmers of this district were; their acreages were large even by prairie standards. The American Red Cross has managed to reconstruct one room for him in a pile of debris which was once a spacious house. There he lives with his old wife, who, during the Hun occupation, became nearly blind and almost completely paralytic. His sons and daughters have been swept beyond his knowledge by the departing armies. Before the Huns left, he had to stand by and watch them uselessly lay waste his home and possessions. His trees are cut down. His barns are laid flat. His cattle are behind the German lines. At the age of seventy, he is starting all afresh and working harder than ever he did in his life. The young architect of the Red Cross visits him often. They sit in the little room of nights, erecting barns and houses more splendid than those that have vanished, but all in the green quiet of the untested future. They shall be standing by the time the captive sons come back.

It is a game at which they play for the sake of the blinded mother; she listens smilingly, nodding her old head, her frail hands folded in her lap.

These pictures which I have painted are typical of some of the things that the American Red Cross is doing. They are isolated examples, which by no means cover all its work. There are the rolling canteens which it has instituted, which follow the French armies. There are the rest houses it has built on the French line of communicat ions for *poilus* who are going on leave or returning. There is the farm for the mutilated, where they are taught to be specialists in certain branches of agriculture, despite their physical curtailments. There is the great campaign against tuberculosis which it is waging. There are its well-conceived warehouses, stored with medical supplies and military and relief necessities, spreading in a great network of usefulness and connected by ambulance transport throughout the whole of the stricken part of France. There are its hospitals, both military and civil. There is the "Lighthouse" for men wounded in battle, founded by Miss Holt in Paris.

I visited this Lighthouse; it is a place infinitely brave and pathetic. Most of the men were picked heroes at the war; they wear their decorations in proof of it. They are greater heroes than ever now. Nothing has more deeply moved me than my few hours among those sightless eyes. In many cases the faces are hideously marred, the eyelids being quite grown together. In several cases besides the eyes, the arms or legs have gone. I have talked and written a good deal about the courage which this war has inspired in ordinary men; but the courage of these blinded men, who once were ordinary, leaves me silent and appalled. They are happy - how and why I cannot understand. Most of them have been taught at the Lighthouse how to overcome their disability and are earning their living as weavers, stenographers, potters, munition-workers. Quite a number of them have families to support. The only complaint that is made against them by their brother-workmen is that they are too rapid; they set too strenuous a pace for the men with eyes. It is a fact that in all trades where sensitiveness of touch is an asset, blindness has increased their efficiency. This is peculiarly so at the Sevres pottery-works where I saw them making the moulds for retorts. A soldier, who was teaching a seeing person Braille, explained his own quickness of perception when he exclaimed, "Ah, madame, it is your eyes which prevent you from seeing!"

I heard some of the stories of the men. There was a captain who, after he had been wounded and while there was yet time to save his sight, insisted on being taken to his General that he might inform him about a German mine. When his mission was completed, his chance of seeing was forever ended.

There was a lieutenant who was blinded in a raid and left for dead out in No Man's Land. Just before he became unconscious, he placed two lumps of earth in line in the direction which led back to his own trenches. He knew the direction by the sound of the retreating footsteps. Whenever he came to himself he groped his way a little nearer to France and before he fainted again, registered the direction with two more lumps of earth placed in line. It took him a day to crawl back.

There was another man who illustrated in a finer way that saying, "It is your eyes which prevent you from seeing." This man before the war was a village-priest, and no credit to his calling. He had a sister who had spent her youth for him and worshipped him beyond everything in the world. He took her adoration brutally for granted. At the outbreak of hostilities he joined the army, serving bravely in the ranks till he was hopelessly blinded. Having always been a thoroughly selfish man, his privation drove him nearly to madness. He had always used the world; now for the first time he had been used by it. His viciousness broke out in blasphemy; he hated both God and man. He made no distinction between people in the mass and the people who tried to help him. His whole desire was to inflict as much pain as he himself suffered. When his sister came to visit him, he employed every ingenuity of word and gesture to cause her agony. Do what she would, he refused to allow her love either to reach or comfort him. She was only a simple peasant woman. In her grief and loneliness she thought matters out and arrived at what seemed to her a practical solution. On her next visit to the hospital she asked to see the doctor. She was taken to him and made her request. "I love my brother," she said; "I have always given him everything. He has lost his eyes and he cannot endure it. Because I love him, I could bear it better. I have been thinking, and I am sure it is possible: I want you to remove my eyes and to put them into his empty sockets."

When the priest was told of her offer, he laughed derisively at her for a fool. Then the reason she had given for her intended sacrifice was told to him, "Because I love him, I could bear it better." He fell silent. All that day he refused food; in the eternal darkness, muffled by his bandages, he was arriving at the truth: she had been willing to suffer what he was now suffering, because she loved him. The hand of love would have made the burden bearable and, if for her, why not for himself? At last, after years of refusal, the simplicity of her tenderness reached and touched him. Presently he was discharged from hospital and taken in hand by the teachers of the blind, who taught him to play the organ. One day his sister came and led him back to his village-parish. Before the war, by his example, he was a danger to God and man; now he sets a very human example of sainthood, labouring without ceasing for others more fortunate than himself. He has increased his efficiency for service by his blindness. Of him it is absolutely true that it was his eyes that prevented him from seeing - from seeing the splendour that lay hidden in himself, no less than in his fellow creatures.

So far I have sketched in the main what the war of compassion is doing for the repatries - the captured French civilians sent back from Germany - and for the refugees of the devastated areas, who have either returned to their ruined farms and villages or were abandoned as useless when the Hun retired. To complete the picture it remains to describe what is being done for the civilian population which has always lived in the battle area of the French armies.

The question may be asked why civilians have been allowed to live here. Curiously enough it is due to the extraordinary humanity of the French Government which makes allowances for the almost religious attachment of the peasant to his tiny plot of land; it is an attachment which is as instinctive and fiercely jealous as that of a cat for her young. He will endure shelling, gassing and all the horrors that scientific invention has produced; he will see his cottage and his barns shattered by bombs and siege-guns, but he will not leave the fields that he has tilled and toiled over, unless he is driven out at the point of the bayonet. I have been told, though I have never seen it, that behind quiet parts of the line, French peasants will gather in their harvest actually in full sight of the Hun. Shells may be falling, but they go stolidly on with their work. There is another reason for this leniency of the Government: they have enough refugees on their hands already and are not going in search of further trouble, until the trouble is forced upon them by circumstances.

As may be imagined, these people live under physical conditions that are terrible. They consist for the most part of women and children; the women are over-worked and the children are neglected. Skin diseases and vermin abound. Clothes are negligible. Washing is a forgotten luxury. Much havoc is wrought by asphyxiating gases which drift across the front-line into the back-country. To the adults are issued protective masks like those that the soldiers wear, but the children do not know how to use them. Many of them are orphans, and live like little animals on roots and offal; for shelter they seek holes in the ground. The American Red Cross is specialising on its efforts to reclaim these children, realising that whatever happens to the adults, the children are the hope of the world.

The part of the Front to which I went to study this work was made famous in 1914 by the disembowellings, shootings and unspeakable indecencies that were perpetrated there. Near by is the little village in which Sister Julie risked her life by refusing to allow her wounded to be butchered. She wears the Legion of Honour now. In the same neighbourhood there lives a Mayor who, after having seen his young wife murdered, protected her murderers from the lynch-law of the mob when next day the town was recaptured. In the same district there is a meadow where fifteen old men were done to death, while a Hun officer sat under an oak-tree, drinking mocking toasts to the victims of each new execution.

The influence of more than three years of warfare has not been elevating, as far as these peasants are concerned. As early as July, a little over a month from its arrival in France, an S.O.S. was sent out by the Prefet of the department, begging the American Red Cross to come and help. In addition to the refugees of old standing, 350 children had been suddenly put into his care. He had nothing but a temporary shelter for them and his need for assistance was acute. Within a few hours the Red Cross had despatched eight workers - a doctor, nurse, bacteriologist, an administrative director and two women to take charge of the bedding, food and clothing. A camionette loaded with condensed milk and other relief necessities was sent by road. On the arrival of the party, they found the children herded together in old barracks, dirty and unfurnished, with no sanitary appliances whatsoever. The sick were crowded together with the well. Of the 350 children, twenty-one were under one year of age, and the rest between one and eight years. The reason for this sudden crisis was that the Huns were bombing the villages behind the lines with asphyxiating gas. The military authorities had therefore withdrawn all children who were too young to adjust their masks themselves, at the same time urging their mothers to carry on the patriotic duty of gathering in the harvest. It was the machinery of mercy which had been built up in six months about this nucleus of eight persons that I set out to visit.

The roads were crowded with the crack troops of France - the Foreign Legion, the Tailleurs, the Moroccans - all marching in one direction, eastward to the trenches. There were rumours of something immense about to happen - no one knew quite what. Were we going to put on a new offensive or were we going to resist one? Many answers were given: they were all guesswork. Meanwhile, our progress was slow; we were continually halting to let brigades of artillery and regiments of infantry pour into the main artery of traffic from lanes and side-roads. When we had backed our car into hedges to give them room to pass, we watched the sea of faces. They were stern and yet laughing, elated and yet childish, eloquent of the love of living and yet familiar with their old friend, Death. They knew that something big was to be demanded of them; before the demand had been made, they had determined to give to the ultimate of their strength. There was a spiritual resolution about their faces which made all their expressions one - the uplifted expression of the unconquered soul of France. That expression blotted out their racial differences. It did not matter that they were Arabs, Negroes, Normans, Parisians; they owned to one nationality - the nationality of martyrdom - and they marched with a single purpose, that freedom might be restored to the world.

When we reached the city to which we journeyed, night had fallen. There was something sinister about our entry; we were veiled in fog, and crept through the gate and beneath the ramparts with extinguished head lights. Scarcely any one was abroad. Those whom we passed, loomed out of the mist in silence, passed stealthily and vanished.

This city is among the most beautiful in France; until recently, although within range of the Hun artillery, it had been left undisturbed. In return the French had spared an equally beautiful city on the other side of the line. This clemency, shown towards two gems of architecture, was the result of one of those silent bargains that are arranged in the language of the guns. But the bargain had been broken by the time I arrived. Bombing planes had been over; the Allied planes had retaliated. Houses, emptied like cart-loads of bricks into the street, were significant of the ruin that was pending. Any moment the orchestra of destruction might break into its overture. Without cessation one could hear a distant booming. The fiddlers of death were tuning up.

Early next morning I went to see the Prefet. He is an old man, whose courage has made him honoured wherever the French tongue is spoken. Others have thought of their own safety and withdrawn into the interior. Never from the start has his sense of duty wavered. Night and day he has laboured incessantly for the refugees, whom he refers to always as "my suffering people." He kept me waiting for some time. Directly I entered he volunteered the explanation: he had just received word from the military authorities that the whole of his civil population must be immediately evacuated. To evacuate a civil population means to tear it up and transplant it root and branch, with no more of its possession than can be carried as hand-baggage. Some 75,000 people would be made homeless directly the Prefet published the order.

It was a dramatic moment, full of tragedy. I glanced out into the square filled with wintry sunlight. I took note of the big gold gates and the monuments. I watched the citizens halting here and there to chat, or going about their errands with a quiet confidence. All this was to be shattered; it had been decided. The same thing was to happen here as had happened at Ypres. The bargain was off. The enemy city, the other side of the line, was to be shelled; this city had to take the consequences. The bargain was off not only as far as the city was concerned, but also as regards its inhabitants' happiness. They had homes to-day; they would be fugitives to-morrow. Then I looked at the old Prefet, who had to break the news to them. He was sitting at his table in his uniform of office, supporting his head in his tired hands.

"What are you going to do?" I asked.

"I have called on the Croix Rouge Americaine to help me," he said. "They have helped me before; they will help me again. These Americans - I have never been to America - but they are my friends. Since they came, they have looked after my babies.

Their doctors and nurses have worked day and night for my suffering people. They are silent; but they do things. There is love in their hands."

While I was still with him the Red Cross officials arrived. They had already wired to Paris. Their lorries and ambulances were converging from all points to meet the emergency. They undertook at once to place all their transport facilities at his disposal. They had started their arrangements for the handling of the children. Extra personnel were being rushed to the spot. There was one unit already in the city. They had hoped to go nearer to the Front, but on arriving had learnt that their permission had been cancelled. It was a bit of luck. They could set to work at once.

I knew this unit and went out to find it. It was composed of American society girls, who had been protected all their lives from ugliness. They had sailed from New York with the vaguest ideas of the war conditions they would encounter; they believed that they were needed to do a nurse-maid's job for France. Their original purpose was to found a creche for the babies of women munition-workers. When they got to Paris they found that such institutions were not wanted. They at once changed their programme, and asked to be allowed to take their creche into the army zone and convert it into a hospital for refugee children. There were interminable delays due to passport formalities - the delays dragged on for three months. During those three months they were called on for no sacrifice; they lived just as comfortably as they had done in New York and, consequently, grew disgusted. They had sailed for France prepared to give something that they had never given before, and France did not seem to want it. At last their passports came; without taking any chances, they got out of Paris and started for the Front. Their haste was well-timed; no sooner had they departed than a message arrived, cancelling their permissions. They had reached the doomed city in which I was at present, two days before its sentence was pronounced. Within four hours of their arrival they had had their first experience of being bombed. Their intention had been to open their hospital in a town still nearer to the front-line. The hospital was prepared and waiting for them. But in the last few days the military situation had changed. A hospital so near the trenches stood a good chance of being destroyed by shell-fire; so once again the unit was held up. It volunteered to abandon its idea of running the hospital for children; it would run it as a first aid hospital for the armies. The offer was refused. These girls, whose gravest interest a year ago had been the season's dances and the latest play, were determined to experience the thrill of sacrifice. So here they were in the doomed city, as the Red Cross officials said, "by luck" - the very place where they were most needed.

When I visited them, after leaving the Prefet's, they had not yet heard that they were to be allowed to stay. They had heard nothing of the city's sentence or of the evacuation of the civil population. All they knew was that the hospital, which had been appointed with their money, was only a few kilometres away and that they were forbidden even to see it. They were gloomy with the fear that within a handful of days they would be again walking the boulevards of Paris. When the news was broken to them of the part they were to play, the full significance of it did not dawn on them at once. "But we don't want anything easy," they complained; "this isn't the Front." "It will be soon," the official told them. When they heard that they cheered up; then their share in the drama was explained. In all probability the city would soon be under constant shell-fire. Refugees would be pouring back from the forward country. The people of the city itself had to be helped to escape before the bombardment commenced. They would have to stay there taking care of the children, packing them into lorries, driving ambulances, rendering first aid, taking the wounded and decrepit out of danger and always returning to it again themselves. As the certainty of the risk and service was impressed on them their faces brightened. Risk and service, that was what they most desired; they were girls, but they hungered to play a soldier's part. They had only dreamt of serving when they had sailed from New York. Those three months of waiting had stung their pride. It was in Paris that the dream of risk had commenced. They would make France want them. Their chance had come.

When I came out into the streets again the word was spreading. Carts were being loaded in front of houses. Everything on wheels, from wagons to perambulators, was being piled up. Everything on four legs, dogs, cattle, horses, was being harnessed and made to do its share in hauling. We left the city, going back to the next point where the refugees would be cared for. On either side of the road, as far as eye could stretch, trenches had been dug, barricades thrown up, blockades and wire-entanglements constructed. It all lay very quiet beneath the sunlight. It seemed a kind of preposterous pretence. One could not imagine these fields as a scene of battle, sweating torture and agony and death. I looked back at the city, one of the most beautiful in France, growing hazy in the distance with its spires and its ramparts. Impossible! Then I remembered the carts being hurriedly loaded and the uplifted faces of those American girls. Where had I seen their expression before? Yes. Strange that they should have caught it! Their expression was the same as that which I had noticed on the Tailleurs, the Foreign Legion and the Moroccans - the crack troops of France.... So they had become that already! At the first hint of danger, their courage had taken command; they had risen into soldiers.

Through villages swarming with troops and packed with ordnance we arrived at an old caserne, which has been converted into the children's hospital of the district. It is in charge of one of the first of America's children's specialists. While he works among the refugees, his wife, who is a sculptress, makes masks for the facially mutilated. He has brought with him from the States some of his students, but his staff is in the main cosmopolitan. One of his nurses is an Australian, who was caught at the outbreak of hostilities in Austria and because of her knowledge, despite her nationality, was allowed to help to organise the Red Cross work of the enemy. Another is a French woman who wears the Croix de Guerre with the palm. She saved her wounded from the fury of the Hun when her village was lost, and helped to get them back to safety after it had been recaptured. The Matron is Swedish and Belgian. The ambulance-drivers are some of the American boys who saw service with the French armies. In this group of workers there are as many stories as there are nationalities.

If the workers have their stories, so have the five hundred little patients. This barrack, converted into a hospital, is full of babies, the youngest being only six days old when I was there. Many of the children have no parents. Others have lost their mothers; their fathers are serving in the trenches. It is not always easy to find out how they became orphans; there are such plentiful chances of losing parents who live continually under shell-fire. One little boy on being asked where his mother was, replied gravely, "My Mama, she is dead. Les Boches, they put a gun to 'er 'ead. She is finished; I 'ave no Mama."

The unchildlike stoicism of these children is appalling. I spent two days among them and heard no crying. Those who are sick, lie motionless as waxen images in their cots. Those who are supposedly well, sit all day brooding and saying nothing. When first they arrive, their faces are earth-coloured. The first thing they have to be taught is how to be children. They have to be coaxed and induced to play; even then they soon grow weary. They seem to regard mere playing as frivolous and indecorous; and so it is in the light of the tragedies they have witnessed. Children of seven have seen more of horror in three years than most old men have read about in a life-time. Many of them have been captured by and recaptured from the Huns. They have been in villages where the dead lay in piles and not even the women were spared. They have been present while indecencies were worked upon their mothers. They have seen men hanged, shot, bayoneted and flung to roast in burning houses. The pictures of all these things hang in their eyes. When they play, it is out of politeness to the kind Americans; not because they derive any pleasure from it.

Night is the troublesome time. The children hide under their beds with terror. The nurses have to go the rounds continually. If the children would only cry, they would give warning. But instead, they creep silently out from between the sheets and crouch against the floor like dumb animals. Dumb animals! That is what they are when first they are brought in. Their most primitive instincts for the beginnings of cleanliness seem to have vanished. They have been fished out of caves, ruined dug-outs, broken houses. They are as full of skin-diseases as the beggar who sat outside Dives' gate, only they have had no dogs to lick their sores. They have lived on offal so long that they have the faces of the extremely aged. And their hatred! Directly you utter the word "Boche," all the little night-gowned figures sit up in their cots and curse. When they have done cursing, of their own accord, they sing the Marseillaise.

Surely if God listens to prayers of vengeance, He will answer the husky petitions of these victims of Hun cruelty! The quiet, just, deep-seated venom of these babies will work the Hun more harm than many batteries. Their fathers come back from the trenches to see them. On leaving, they turn to the American nurses, "We shall fight better now," they say, "because we know that you are taking care of them."

When those words are spoken, the American Red Cross knows that it is achieving its object and is winning its war of compassion. The whole drive of all its effort is to win the war in the shortest possible space of time. It is in Europe to save children for the future, to re-kindle hope in broken lives, to mitigate the toll of unavoidable suffering, but first and foremost to help men to fight better.

Coningsby Dawson

IV

THE LAST WAR

The last war! I heard the phrase for the first time on the evening after Great Britain had declared war. I was in Quebec en route for England, wondering whether my ship was to be allowed to sail. There had been great excitement all day, bands playing the Marseillaise, Frenchmen marching arm-in-arm singing, orators, gesticulating and haranguing from balconies, street-corners and the base of statues.

Now that the blue August night was falling and every one was released from work, the excitement was redoubled. Quebec was finding in war an opportunity for carnival. Throughout all the pyramided city the Tri-colour and the Union Jack were waving. At the foot of the Heights, the broad basin of the St. Lawrence was a-drift in the dusk with fluttering pennons. They looked like homing birds, settling in dovecotes of the masts and rigging.

As night deepened, Chinese lanterns were lighted and carried on poles through the narrow streets. Troops of merry-makers followed them, blowing horns, dragging bells, tin-cans, anything that would make a noise and express high spirits. They linked arms with girls as they marched and were lost, laughing in the dusk. If a French reservist could be found who was sailing in the first ship bound for the slaughter, he became the hero of the hour and was lifted shoulder high at the head of the procession. War was a brave game at which to play. This was to be a short war and a merry one. Down with the Germans! Up with France! Hurrah for the entente cordiale!

Beneath the coronet of stars on the Heights of Abraham the spirit of Wolfe kept watch and brooded. It was under these circumstances, that I heard the phrase for the first time - *the last war.*

The street was blocked with a gaping crowd. All the faces were raised to an open window, two storeys up, from which the frame had been taken out. Inside the building one could hear the pounding of machinery, for it was here that the most important paper of Quebec was printed. Across a huge white sheet a man on a hanging platform painted the latest European cables. A cluster of electric lights illuminated him strongly; but he was not the centre of the crowd's attention. In the window stood another man. Like myself he was waiting for his ship to sail, but not to England - to France. He was a returning French reservist. Across the many miles of ocean the hand of duty had stretched and touched him; he was ecstatically glad that he was wanted. In those first days this ecstasy of gladness was a little hard to understand. Thank God we all share it instinctively now. He was speaking excitedly, addressing the crowd. They cheered him; they were in a mood to cheer anybody. His face was thin with earnestness; he was a spirit-man. He waved aside their applause with impatience. He was trying to inspire them with his own intensity. In the intervals between the shouting, I caught some of his words, "I am setting out to fight the last war - the war of humanity which will bring universal peace and friendship to the world."

A sailor behind me spat. He was drunk and feeling the need of sympathy. He began to explain to me the reason. He was a fireman on one of the steamers in the basin and a reservist in the British Navy. He had received his orders that day to report back in England for duty; he knew that he was going to be torpedoed on his voyage across the Atlantic. How did he know? He had had a vision. Sailors always had visions before they were drowned. It was to combat this vision that he had got drunk.

I shook him off irritably. One didn't require the superstitions of an alcoholic imagination to emphasize the new terror which had overtaken the world. There was enough of fear in the air already. All this spurious gaiety - what was it? Nothing but the chatter of lonely children who were afraid to listen to the silence - afraid lest they might hear the creaking footstep of death upon the stairs. And these candles, lighting up the fringes of the night - they were nothing but a vain pretence that the darkness had not gathered.

But this spirit-man framed in the window, he was genuine and different. Yesterday we should have passed him in the street unnoticed; to-day the mantle of prophecy clothed him. Within two months he might be dead - horribly dead with a bayonet through him. That thought was in the minds of all who watched him; it gave him an added authority. Yet he was not thinking of himself, of wounds, of death; he was not even thinking of France. He was thinking of humanity: "I am setting out to fight the last war - the war of humanity which will bring universal peace and friendship to the world."

Since the war started, how often have we heard that phrase - *the last war!* It became the battle-cry of all recruiting-men, who would have fought under no other circumstances, joined up now so that this might be the final carnage. Nations left their desks and went into battle voluntarily, long before self-interest forced them, simply because organised murder so disgusted them that they were determined by weight of numbers to make this exhibition of brutality the last.

Before Europe burst into flames in 1914, we believed that the last war had been already fought. The most vivid endorsement of this belief came out of Germany in a book which, to my mind, up to that time was the strongest peace-argument in modern literature. It was so strong that the Kaiser's Government had the author arrested and every copy that could be found destroyed. Nevertheless, over a million were secretly printed and circulated in Germany, and it was translated into every major European language. The book I refer to was known under its American title as, *The Human Slaughter-House*. It told very simply how men who had played the army game of sticking dummies, found themselves called upon to stick their brother-men; how they obeyed at first, then sickened at sight of their own handiwork, until finally the rank and file on both sides flung down their arms, banded themselves together and refused to carry out the orders of their generals. There was no declaration of peace; in that moment national boundaries were abolished.

In 1912 this sounded probable. I remember the American press-comments. They all agreed that national prejudices had been broken down to such an extent by socialism and friendly intercourse, that never again would statesmen be able to launch attacks of nations against nations. Governments might declare war; the peoples whom they governed would merely overthrow them. The world had become too common-sense to commit murder on so vast a scale.

Had it? The world in general might have: but Germany had not. The argument of *The Human Slaughter-House* proposed by a German in protest against what he foresaw was surely coming, turned out to be a bad guess. It made no allowance for what happens when a mad dog starts running through the world. One may be tender-hearted. One may not like killing dogs. One may even be an anti-vivisectionist; but when a dog is mad, the only humanitarian thing to do is to kill it. If you don't, the women and children pay the penalty.

We have had our illustration in Russia of what occurs when one side flings away its arms, practising the idealistic reasonings which this book propounds: the more brutal side conquers. While the Blonde Beast runs abroad spreading rabies, the only idealist who counts is the idealist who carries a rifle on his shoulder - the only gospel to which the world listens is the gospel which saviours are dying for.

The last war! It took us all by surprise. We had believed so utterly in peace; now we had to prove our faith by being prepared to die for it. If we did not die, this war would not be the last; it would be only the preface to the next. To paraphrase the words of Mr. Wells, "We had been prepared to take life in a certain way and life had taken us, as it takes every generation, in an entirely different way. We had been prepared to be altruistic pacifists, and ..."

And here we are, in this year of 1918, engaged upon the bloodiest war of all time, harnessing the muscle and brain-power of the universe to one end - that we may contrive new and yet more deadly methods of butchering our fellow men. The men whom we kill, we do not hate individually. The men whom we kill, we do not see when they are dead. We scald them with liquid fire; we stifle them with gas; we drop volcanoes on them from the clouds; we pull firing-levers three, ten, even fifteen miles away and hurl them into eternity unconfessed. And this we do with pity in our hearts, both for them and for ourselves. And why? Because they have given us no choice. They have promised, unless we defend ourselves, to snatch our souls from us and fashion them afresh into souls which shall bear the stamp of their own image. Of their souls we have seen samples; they date back to the dark ages - the souls of Cain, Judas and Caesar Borgia were not unlike them. Of what such souls are capable they have given us examples in Belgium, captured France and in the living dead whom they return by way of Evian. We would rather forego our bodies than so exchange our souls. A Germanised world is like a glimpse of madness; the very thought strikes terror to the heart. Yet it is to Germanise the world that Germany is waging war to-day - that she may confer upon us the benefits of her own proved swinishness. There is nothing left for us but to fight for our souls like men.

The last war! We believed that at first, but as the years dragged on the certainty became an optimism, the optimism a dream which we well-nigh knew to be impossible. We have always known that we would beat Germany - we have never doubted that. But could we beat her so thoroughly that she would never dare to reperpetrate this horror? Could we prove to her that war is not and never was a paying way of conducting business? Men began to smile when we spoke of this war as the last. "There have always been wars," they said; "this one is not the last - there will be others."

If it is not to be the last, we have cheated ourselves. We have cheated the men who have died for us. Our chief ideal in fighting is taken away. Many a lad who moulders in a stagnant trench, laid down his life for this sole purpose, that no children of the future ages should have to pass through his Gethsemane. He consciously gave himself up as a scapegoat, that the security of human sanity should be safeguarded against a recurrence of this enormity. The spirit-man, framed in the dusky window above the applauding crowds in Quebec, was typical of all these men who have made the supreme sacrifice. His words utter the purpose that was in all their hearts, "I am setting out to fight the last war - the war of humanity which will bring universal peace and freedom to the world."

That promise was becoming a lie; it is capable of fulfilment now. The dream became possible in April, 1917, when America took up her cross of martyrdom. Great Britain, France and the United States, the three great promise-keeping nations, are standing side by side. They together, if they will when the war is ended, can build an impregnable wall for peace about the world. The plunderer who knew that it was not Great Britain, nor France, nor America, but all three of them united as Allies that he had to face, no matter how tempted he was to prove that armed force meant big business, would be persuaded to expand his commerce by more legitimate methods. Whether this dream is to be accomplished will be decided not upon any battlefield but in the hearts of the civilians of all three countries - particularly in those of America and Great Britain. The soldiers who have fought and suffered together, can never be anything but friends.

My purpose in writing this account of America in France has

been to give grounds for understanding and appreciation; it has been to prove that the highest reward that either America or Great Britain can gain as a result of its heroism is an Anglo-American alliance, which will fortify the world against all such future terrors. There never ought to have been anything but alliance between my two great countries. They speak the same tongue, share a common heritage and pursue the same loyalties. Had we not blundered in our destinies, there would never have been occasion for anything but generosity.

The opportunity for generosity has come again. Any man or woman who, whether by design or carelessness, attempts to mar this growing friendship is perpetrating a crime against humanity as grave as that of the first armed Hun who stepped across the Belgian threshold. It were better for them that mill-stones were hung about their necks and they were cast into the sea, than ...

God is giving us our chance. The magnanimities of the Anglo-Saxon races are rising to greet one another. If those magnanimities are welcomed and made permanent, our soldier-idealists will not have died in vain. Then we shall fulfil for them their promise, "We are setting out to fight the last war."

Choose from Thousands of 1stWorldLibrary Classics By

A. M. Barnard
Ada Leverson
Adolphus William Ward
Aesop
Agatha Christie
Alexander Aaronsohn
Alexander Kielland
Alexandre Dumas
Alfred Gatty
Alfred Ollivant
Alice Duer Miller
Alice Turner Curtis
Alice Dunbar
Ambrose Bierce
Amelia E. Barr
Amory H. Bradford
Andrew Lang
Andrew McFarland Davis
Andy Adams
Anna Sewell
Annie Besant
Annie Hamilton Donnell
Annie Payson Call
Annonaymous
Anton Chekhov
Arnold Bennett
Arthur Conan Doyle
Arthur M. Winfield
Arthur Ransome
Atticus
B.H. Baden-Powell
B. M. Bower
Baroness Emmuska Orczy
Baroness Orczy
Basil King
Bayard Taylor
Ben Macomber
Bertha Muzzy Bower
Bjornstjerne Bjornson
Booth Tarkington
Boyd Cable
Bram Stoker
C. Collodi
C. E. Orr
C. M. Ingleby
Carolyn Wells
Catherine Parr Traill
Charles A. Eastman
Charles Dickens

Charles Dudley Warner
Charles Farrar Browne
Charles Ives
Charles Kingsley
Charles Klein
Charles Amory Beach
Charles Hanson Towne
Charles Lathrop Pack
Charles Whibley
Charles Willing Beale
Charlotte M. Braeme
Charlotte M. Yonge
Charlotte Perkins Stetson
Clair W. Hayes
Clarence Day Jr.
Clarence E. Mulford
Clemence Housman
Confucius
Cornelis DeWitt Wilcox
Cyril Burleigh
D. H. Lawrence
Daniel Defoe
David Garnett
Dinah Craik
Don Carlos Janes
Donald Keyhoe
Dorothy Kilner
Dougan Clark
Douglas Fairbanks
E. Nesbit
E.P.Roe
E. Phillips Oppenheim
Earl Barnes
Edgar Rice Burroughs
Edith Van Dyne
Edith Wharton
Edward J. O'Biren
Edward S. Ellis
Edwin L. Arnold
Eleanor Atkins
Eliot Gregory
Elizabeth Gaskell
Elizabeth McCracken
Elizabeth Von Arnim
Ellem Key
Emerson Hough
Emilie F. Carlen
Emily Dickinson
Enid Bagnold

Enilor Macartney Lane
Erasmus W. Jones
Ernie Howard Pie
Ethel Turner
Ethel Watts Mumford
Eugenie Foa
Eugene Wood
Eustace Hale Ball
Evelyn Everett-green
Everard Cotes
F. H. Cheley
F. J. Cross
Federick Austin Ogg
Ferdinand Ossendowski
Francis Bacon
Francis Darwin
Frances Hodgson Burnett
Frances Parkinson Keyes
Frank Gee Patchin
Frank Harris
Frank Jewett Mather
Frank L. Packard
Frank V. Webster
Frederic Stewart Isham
Frederick Trevor Hill
Frederick Winslow Taylor
Friedrich Kerst
Friedrich Nietzsche
Fyodor Dostoyevsky
G.A. Henty
G.K. Chesterton
Gabrielle E. Jackson
Garrett P. Serviss
Gaston Leroux
George A. Warren
George Ade
Geroge Bernard Shaw
George Durston
George Ebers
George Eliot
George Gissing
George MacDonald
George Meredith
George Orwell
George Sylvester Viereck
George Tucker
George W. Cable
George Wharton James
Gertrude Atherton

Grace E. King
Grace Gallatin
Grant Allen
Guillermo A. Sherwell
Gulielma Zollinger
Gustav Flaubert
H. A. Cody
H. B. Irving
H.C. Bailey
H. G. Wells
H. H. Munro
H. Irving Hancock
H. Rider Haggard
H. W. C. Davis
Hamilton Wright Mabie
Hans Christian Andersen
Harold Avery
Harold McGrath
Harriet Beecher Stowe
Harry Houidini
Helent Hunt Jackson
Helen Nicolay
Hendrik Conscience
Hendy David Thoreau
Henri Barbusse
Henrik Ibsen
Henry Adams
Henry Ford
Henry Frost
Henry James
Henry Jones Ford
Henry Seton Merriman
Henry W Longfellow
Herbert A. Giles
Herbert N. Casson
Herman Hesse
Homer
Honore De Balzac
Horace Walpole
Horatio Alger Jr.
Howard Pyle
Howard R. Garis
Hugh Lofting
Hugh Walpole
Humphry Ward
Ian Maclaren
Inez Haynes Gillmore
Irving Bacheller
Israel Abrahams
Ivan Turgenev
J.G.Austin

J. Henri Fabre
J. M. Barrie
J. Macdonald Oxley
J. S. Fletcher
J. S. Knowles
J. Storer Clouston
Jack London
Jacob Abbott
James Allen
James Andrews
James Baldwin
James DeMille
James Joyce
James Lane Allen
James Lane Allen
James Oliver Curwood
James Oppenheim
James Otis
James R. Driscoll
Jane Austen
Janet Aldridge
Jens Peter Jacobsen
Jerome K. Jerome
John Burroughs
John Cournos
John F. Kennedy
John Gay
John Glasworthy
John Habberton
John Joy Bell
John Kendrick Bangs
John Milton
John Philip Sousa
Jonas Lauritz Idemil Lie
Jonathan Swift
Joseph A. Altsheler
Joseph Carey
Joseph Conrad
Joseph E. Badger Jr
Joseph Hergesheimer
Joseph Jacobs
Jules Vernes
Julian Hawthrone
Julie A Lippmann
Justin Huntly McCarthy
Kakuzo Okakura
Kenneth Grahame
Kenneth McGaffey
Kate Langley Bosher
Kate Langley Bosher
Katherine Cecil Thurston

Katherine Stokes
L. A. Abbot
L. T. Meade
L. Frank Baum
Latta Griswold
Laura Lee Hope
Laurence Housman
Lawrence Beasley
Leo Tolstoy
Leonid Andreyev
Lewis Carroll
Lewis Sperry Chafer
Lilian Bell
Lloyd Osbourne
Louis Hughes
Louis Tracy
Louisa May Alcott
Lucy Fitch Perkins
Lucy Maud Montgomery
Lydia Miller Middleton
Lyndon Orr
M. Corvus
M. H. Adams
Margaret E. Sangster
Margaret Vandercook
Margret Penrose
Maria Edgeworth
Maria Thompson Daviess
Mariano Azuela
Marion Polk Angellotti
Mark Overton
Mark Twain
Mary Austin
Mary Catherine Crowley
Mary Cole
Mary Hastings Bradley
Mary Roberts Rinehart
Mary Rowlandson
M. Wollstonecraft Shelley
Maud Lindsay
Max Beerbohm
Myra Kelly
Nathaniel Hawthrone
Nicolo Machiavelli
O. F. Walton
Oscar Wilde
Owen Johnson
P.G. Wodehouse
Paul and Mabel Thorne
Paul G. Tomlinson
Paul Severing

Percy Brebner
Peter B. Kyne
Plato
R. Derby Holmes
R. L. Stevenson
R. S. Ball
Rabindranath Tagore
Rahul Alvares
Ralph Bonehill
Ralph Henry Barbour
Ralph Victor
Ralph Waldo Emmerson
Rene Descartes
Rex Beach
Rex E. Beach
Richard Harding Davis
Richard Jefferies
Richard Le Gallienne
Robert Barr
Robert Frost
Robert Gordon Anderson
Robert L. Drake
Robert Lansing
Robert Lynd
Robert Michael Ballantyne
Robert W. Chambers
Rosa Nouchette Carey
Rudyard Kipling
Samuel B. Allison

Samuel Hopkins Adams
Sarah Bernhardt
Sarah C. Hallowell
Selma Lagerlof
Sherwood Anderson
Sigmund Freud
Standish O'Grady
Stanley Weyman
Stella Benson
Stephen Crane
Stewart Edward White
Stijn Streuvels
Swami Abhedananda
Swami Parmananda
T. S. Ackland
T. S. Arthur
The Princess Der Ling
Thomas A. Janvier
Thomas A Kempis
Thomas Anderton
Thomas Bailey Aldrich
Thomas Bulfinch
Thomas De Quincey
Thomas H. Huxley
Thomas Hardy
Thomas More
Thornton W. Burgess
U. S. Grant
Valentine Williams

Various Authors
Vaughan Kester
Victor Appleton
Virginia Woolf
Walter Camp
Walter Scott
Washington Irving
Wilbur Lawton
Wilkie Collins
Willa Cather
Willard F. Baker
William Dean Howells
William le Queux
W. Makepeace Thackeray
William W. Walter
Winston Churchill
Yei Theodora Ozaki
Yogi Ramacharaka
Young E. Allison
Zane Grey

www.ingramcontent.com/pod-product-compliance
Lightning Source LLC
Chambersburg PA
CBHW051851170626
46807CB00003B/1434